AF413556

"In an age of AI—when what we crave most is real humanity—Glenn Bostock's Human Business model reminds us of what so many corporations have lost: the simple powers of caring, connection, and purpose. This book shows that being truly human isn't just idealistic; it's essential for creating workplaces where people can genuinely thrive."

—SUSIE OGIHARA

Strategic Project Manager, Panasonic R&D Company of North America

"*A Human Business* shows, through real stories and experience, that businesses work best when people truly come first. Respect, purpose, and care aren't soft ideas, they are practical principles that build strong, resilient companies. It's a timely reminder that when you focus on serving the customer and respecting the people doing the work, everything else follows."

—RYAN TIERNEY

Managing Director, Sperrin Metal; Founder, Lean Made Simple

"No fluff here—Glenn shares the practical blueprint from his lifelong experiential learning discovering the cultural DNA best suited to see a Human Business thrive! His insights into creating a business system where people flourish through meaningful work will help companies be more innovative, resilient, and profitable."

—MARC KUZIK

Board Member, Association for Manufacturing Excellence

"As a friend and admirer of Glenn, his personal growth and success are heartwarming. The message in this book is powerful for all who believe and strive for continuous growth in their personal and career lives."

—DICK BRICKMAN
CEO, The Brickman Group

"Glenn's perspective on workplace culture—rooted in genuine connection, trust, and supporting people—is exactly the approach businesses need for lasting success. We share these values by strengthening both leaders and employee growth with emotional intelligence. His message resonated deeply and inspired our community to take action."

—JENNEFER GRIFFITH
Executive Director, Food Processing Skills Canada

"*A Human Business* is a refreshing reminder that work doesn't have to drain us. This book shows how caring for people first creates healthier teams, stronger businesses, and more meaningful lives."

—JOSH BARNES
Owner, Barnes Welding Inc.

"Glenn Bostock possesses a rare quality of leadership: the ability to transform adversity into opportunity with genuine conviction. In *A Human Business*, he shows readers how challenges serve as powerful invitations for innovation, growth, and the opportunity to create solutions. Glenn has proven these principles, not only on these pages, but through his own distinguished career."

—PETER RHODES
Author, *Observing Spirit*

"In a business world where artificial intelligence and industrial robots are threatening to replace human interaction and genuine caring, *A Human Business* has arrived at exactly the right time. It is a breakthrough blueprint that eloquently and movingly describes the timeless principles that should guide ethical enterprise."

—RAY SILVERMAN, PHD

Professor Emeritus of Religion and English, Bryn Athyn College; author of the introduction to Helen Keller's *How I Would Help the World*

"*A Human Business* is a powerful reminder that companies are, first and foremost, communities of people. The book inspires readers to once again see work as a place of purpose, responsibility, and mutual support."

—JAN-MICHEL SCHÜSLER

Lean Project Manager, Tridelta Meidensha GmbH

"Glenn Bostock is a creative, inquisitive, self-examining, and self-aware entrepreneur whose vision for his company has always been forward-thinking, unique, productive, efficient, and compassionate. From all the improvements he has made over the decades, comes this metaphor of a business needing to be a human business. Read *A Human Business* to learn new business concepts, cultivate out-of-the-box thinking, and inspire your leadership vision."

—SUSAN B. SMITH

Founder and president, LooptyHoops; Chair emeritus, Vistage Worldwide

"*A Human Business* reflects Glenn Bostock's uncommon ability to unite disciplined business thinking with genuine care for people. It is practical, grounded, and shaped by decades of lived leadership."

—BRUCE HAMILTON

Sr. Advisor, GBMP Consulting Group

A HUMAN BUSINESS

GLENN BOSTOCK

Founder & CEO of SnapCab

A HUMAN BUSINESS

THE PEOPLE-FIRST MODEL FOR LASTING *SUCCESS*

Forbes | Books

Published by Forbes Books, Charleston, South Carolina.
An imprint of Advantage Media Group.

Forbes Books is a registered trademark, and the Forbes Books colophon is a trademark of Forbes Media, LLC.

Printed in the United States of America.

10 9 8 7 6 5 4 3 2 1

ISBN: 979-8-88750-797-2 (Hardcover)
ISBN: 979-8-88750-798-9 (eBook)
ISBN: 979-8-88750-799-6 (Audiobook)

Library of Congress Control Number: 2026902279

Cover art and graphics by Jenn Emon.

This custom publication is intended to provide accurate information and the opinions of the author in regard to the subject matter covered. It is sold with the understanding that the publisher, Forbes Books, is not engaged in rendering legal, financial, or professional services of any kind. If legal advice or other expert assistance is required, the reader is advised to seek the services of a competent professional.

Since 1917, Forbes has remained steadfast in its mission to serve as the defining voice of entrepreneurial capitalism. Forbes Books, launched in 2016 through a partnership with Advantage Media, furthers that aim by helping business and thought leaders bring their stories, passion, and knowledge to the forefront in custom books. Opinions expressed by Forbes Books authors are their own. To be considered for publication, please visit **books.Forbes.com**.

02-05-2026 1:45

*To Peter Rhodes, for being the person who made me
wake up to my human condition.*

The core of a Human Business is building a foundation of caring that includes embracing each other's strengths and weaknesses, utilizing what each of us loves to do to help maximize our usefulness at work and our purpose in life.
—GLENN BOSTOCK

CONTENTS

ACKNOWLEDGMENTS

would like to thank my wife, Cheryl Bostock, for her partnership and for her long-standing support of my passion for business. I would like to thank my dad, Peter Bostock, who believed in me from the beginning and who introduced me to the elevator remodeling industry. I would like to acknowledge my friend, Greg Glebe, for his friendship all these years. I would like to thank my childhood tutors, Jane Beebe and Donnette Alfelt. Thank you to my mentors, Peter Rhodes, Ray Silverman, and Dick Brickman. Thank you to my Vistage Chair, Susan Smith, and my Vistage friends. Thank you to my editors: Stephen Ahlberg, Heather Adams, Kendall Hyatt, Michelle Rose, and Carla Bostock. I would like to thank Jenn Emon for the graphics and the book cover. Most especially, thank you to my SnapCab community and my leadership team: Sahiza Hossenbaccus, John Richards, Joe Danko, Jon Kerr, Patty Greenawalt, Micah Alden, and Jennifer Lahtaw—you are my colleagues, teammates, and friends. A special thanks to my executive assistant, Susan Lahtaw, who makes it possible for me to function every day. We are a company of over 150 people at the writing of this book, and everybody has played a role in *A Human Business*. I value each and every one of you. You are the humans who make up a Human Business, a model for others to follow.

Business exists to serve humanity—not to exploit it. True success comes from fulfilling real needs with integrity, not chasing profit. Choose service over greed, and help build a better world.
—GLENN BOSTOCK

In the fifty years I spent leading South Mountain Company, and in the few years since, I have written and spoken extensively about this employee-owned enterprise.

Much of what Glenn Bostock says in this new book fully resonates with my own business experience. And yet, there is so much in *A Human Business* that I have never even begun to articulate. Reading the book, I often found myself saying, "Hey, I could have said that." But I didn't. Glenn did. I love that.

There's a *lot* to love in this book.

The list begins—and ultimately rests on—Glenn's disarming and authentic honesty. The book recognizes pain and trouble as precursors to progress, and it weaves a tale of a journey to overcome fear and missteps. The introspection required to do this has led to innovation and invention. By supporting the people who do the work at SnapCab, Glenn and his team have provided a compelling model.

Glenn invites us into the messy, exhilarating, and vulnerable work of building an organization where people thrive because they are trusted, heard, and held to high standards. He speaks plainly but with conviction, generously without gloss. The result is a fundamental recalibration of doing business—how to do it differently and better.

Glenn champions a notion that many have neglected: that business is, and will always be, about people. He compares a business to a human body, with interactive systems and parts that all play a role. He challenges us to look past spreadsheets and metrics. He shows us the values-driven approach that he has found to be not only ethical but strategic and rewarding.

This leads to the radical notion that treating people well is not the enemy of high performance—it is, in fact, the foundation. That's Human Business. I'll tell a business story from my own experience that I believe exemplifies the spirit of a Human Business, even though it happened long before this book was written.

As it was for so many other small businesses, the economic crash of 2008 was a shock to South Mountain's system. It shook us to the core.

An avalanche of crushing postponements jolted us loose from the petrified status quo that prosperity had layered into our collective company consciousness. It untethered us from our preconceptions about who we were. It became a powerful catalyst that drove us to take a sobering look at what we do, how we do it, and how we might do it better—to insist on the future we wanted.

As we considered creative ways to rebuild our shrinking backlog, it was also our moment to tackle the unthinkable: What happens when the day comes when there is not enough work for all? The examination had surprising results.

Probing, heartfelt discussions led to the following company policy:

> In the event of not enough work to provide full-time employment for all individuals in the company, management will enact the following, in this order:
>
> - Implement voluntary temporary rolling furloughs
> - Employ people doing speculative work (income deferred) for limited periods
> - Employ people doing non-income-producing work for limited periods
> - Strategically reduce hours worked
> - Reduce wages across the board by a percentage
> - Implement involuntary temporary rolling furloughs

The thrilling part of this process was that never, during these difficult discussions, did the word *layoffs* come up. Never did anyone suggest that those who had been with us for less time should be at greater risk. This was a time of coming together, as a workplace community, rather than a time of fragmentation and protection of individual self-interests.

Ultimately, we used each of those strategies at one time or another. I'll never forget the company meeting at which we announced that we were cutting all wages by 20 percent. Several people came up to me afterward and thanked me, right after their wages were cut by 20 percent! "You're losing more than we are," they said. Their gratitude was for a culture of mutual support, for what Glenn calls a Human Business. It's not to say that no one ever gets let go from a Human Business, but just as all parts of a human body work together to solve all manner of health problems, people who share the Human Business values naturally see each other as interdependent.

Looking back, I now say that the crash was the second-best thing that ever happened to us. It was particularly cathartic for me. I'm embarrassed to say that until that crisis, I thought that a fundamental part of my job as a leader was to protect my colleagues and co-owners from stress. How wrong I was. My job, as I came to understand it, was to bring them to the table, share fully, give them the opportunity to solve the problems that were causing the stress, and serve them. It took me too long to learn that valuable lesson.

As you turn these pages, you'll discover more than sound, actionable business strategies. You'll find a whole-cloth philosophy of leadership and collaboration. Whether you're an executive, a manager, a young entrepreneur, or a maker, *A Human Business* will call you to summon what matters most: our shared purpose.

This book is desperately needed in these times when working people have been left so far behind, and when we have come to accept public cruelty, gross corruption, and extreme wealth inequality. The future of business belongs in the hands of those who provide antidotes to the failed model of winners and losers.

I believe that Glenn and I share this perspective. We share something else: We each started in business with a deep passion for woodworking. We each came to learn that crafting a business is not unlike crafting an object of beauty and function out of pieces of wood. But businesses are made not of raw materials but of people, all of whom deserve dignity and respect, meaningful work, and a share of the bounty.

—John Abrams, founder and president emeritus of South Mountain Company and the author of *From Founder to Future: A Business Roadmap to Impact, Longevity, and Employee Ownership* (Berrett-Koehler Publishing, 2025)

While it is difficult to revisit the painful parts of life, I feel compelled to share my story if that means helping other people and contributing to a better work culture in other businesses. A better work atmosphere in organizations means happier people and a better world. So how could I hold back? I've been given so much. Even my shortcomings have led, in a winding path, to my success, which supports so many wonderful employees and their families. Looking back on my life, it was my worst days that led to my best days.

THE PROBLEM WITH ME

Before I was a business owner with four decades of experience, I was a boy in school. And the boy in school had a problem—it was a source of shame, a barrier to joy, something I fought against for years of my life. I was dyslexic, and it was not OK. I had a hard time paying attention. I needed help. It would never be OK to be who I was as a human being—unless I could move past my learning differences. Only then would I find acceptance and be happy in my life and with myself. That is how it was for me as a boy, long before I was the founder and CEO of a successful manufacturing company with two locations in the US and Canada, which, as of the time of this book's publishing, has grown to over 150 employees.

You'll learn the details of my story in this book. You'll watch me grapple with my weaknesses. You'll watch me change from the human being I was then to the human being I am now, having uncovered a mindset that changed the course of my business, which aims to feed our community spirit, fostering goodwill inside each person who is a part of it. In this way, this mindset is not just practical but spiritual.

Can you relate to the kind of thinking I just described? Do you have a weakness that you believe stands in the way of your personal happiness? You discover a flaw in who you are; then you go about using all your energy over the course of months or years to get rid of it. If the problem goes away, you're a success. If it doesn't, there is only one thing to do: Bury it. Toughen up. Fake it. Compensate for it. Keep your problem a secret from the people around you—especially those at work. Resign yourself to just getting by.

But is that what your purpose amounts to—hiding your problem, snuffing your spirit, or just surviving?

THE PROBLEM WITH WORK

In 1970, economist Milton Friedman published a controversial essay in *The New York Times* titled "A Friedman Doctrine—The Social Responsibility of Business Is to Increase Its Profits." He claimed that a company's primary duty was to maximize shareholder profits. While his position had nuances that have been debated over the years, its damaging core message—profit above all else—has been widely embraced by the corporate world for decades. This has arguably led to a decline in the quality of life for both workers and consumers.

Today, many workers are in distress—existing in a toxic day-to-day grind that leaves them drained and purposeless. Maybe "trying to get through the day" didn't start out as your life's purpose. It may be the reality you're dealing with, nevertheless. You might feel empty, burnt-out, or isolated. You're not alone in these feelings. Convention, especially in the business world, requires a loyalty to cultural norms that can undermine who we are at heart. You may be one of the many people waking up each day to a professional environment that demands hardness of heart, hiding, and a big expenditure of personal energy—all for the sake of one driving purpose: making money.

Is this familiar?

THE PROBLEM WITH PROFIT AS PURPOSE

From a business owner's point of view, is the financial motive of a conventional corporation really that bad? Only you can say what's true for you. My own experience of profit as purpose is that its ultimate consequence is an environment that doesn't work. It breeds fear, isolation, and unhealthy competition; it opposes a growing, productive, and happy community. Of course, making money is necessary for any business to provide fair wages and ensure its longevity. However, a focus on being useful—on providing value beyond profit—can have a profoundly positive impact on employees, customers, and even the world at large.

A NEW VISION OF WORK

What if there was an alternative to simply surviving the day? What if there was a different take available on your personal problems, the weaknesses in your closest relationships, and the issues that come up at work? What if you could trade the set of values that tells you to be hard, insincere, and focused on making money for a set of values that tells you to be kind, authentic, and useful?

Whether you are an employee or an employer, I want to invite you into a new environment, a whole new mindset. This one's a bit warmer than you are used to. I want work to feel heavenly, not hellish.

Imagine a community you want to be part of. Picture a setting filled with people and activities that harmonize with who you are and what you want to do. You have a purpose. You are valued not only for your contributions but for the quality of your presence inside the community. You are celebrated not only for achieving your goals but for your enthusiasm and desire to participate in new initiatives. You are encouraged to be honest—about everything—and it's safe to do that. You are given room to trip over your words and find your footing again without fear of thoughtless comments, punishment, or demotion. In fact, you are respected to the extent that you process your problems while continuing to use your personal strengths. You find that, by some miracle, you are not seeking happiness at work but are finding it anyway. Your supply of energy for what you do appears to be unlimited. You are not completely happy without your life at work. **Work is a place where you have the opportunity to be genuinely useful to other people, and you feel the appreciation of those you serve. In essence, you have found a place to exercise your life's purpose.** You have found your own personal heaven.

As a leader, this book gives me the opportunity to share the story of SnapCab's growth and development with my entire team—the next generation of SnapCab leaders—in order to document a shared vision to be referenced for years to come. I can also offer leaders an alternative business model that prioritizes service to the customer—but not at the expense of the human beings who, together, bring to life the organism called the company. In essence, I propose a way to work that makes people want to work. What we know for sure at SnapCab is that we enjoy a satisfying way of life at work that we'd like to pass on to others.

Is it hard to imagine the type of work life I am describing? It is the intent of this book to help you opt out of unfulfilling work as you know it; tap into your own experience of acceptance, joy, and purpose; and find a home at work.

Have you ever been surrounded by a group of friends who made you feel completely supported and at home? A community where you were free to be yourself and not fear rejection, even when you failed? Have you ever been lost in the joy of doing an activity that you love while time passes without you noticing and you enter a "flow state"? Have you seen this flow state benefit others? What if you could combine all these things? Better yet, what if you could experience those things every day at work?

This new vision of work is available to you through the Human Business model presented in this book. A Human Business is a model of community that is analogous to a human body. It is a model of business that reflects the harmony that results when all organ systems—parts of a company—operate in service of a common intention.

As founder and CEO of SnapCab—a multimillion-dollar business that has been in operation for forty years—I have gained valuable insight on how to run a successful business. It may sound counterintuitive, but I have stopped thinking about profit first. Instead, my first priority is to create a culture of caring. Why? It builds a community of colleagues who enjoy working together; it builds loyal customers who want to see the company succeed; and it builds a sense of satisfaction that you're contributing something useful to the world. This approach attracts good people—customers, employees, and partners alike—and, yes, it leads to profit and longevity.

OUR COMPANY INTENTION AND THE HUMAN FORM

The various components of a business must work together so it not only stays alive but also thrives. The interconnected nature of this principle is much like the different parts of a human body. At SnapCab, a company that specializes in designing and manufacturing elevator interiors and custom privacy pod products, thriving means bringing to life our company intention: **to create communities of usefulness** for our customers and for our own team. What exactly is usefulness? It is helpfulness, harmony, and providing value. Usefulness is constructive activity that is connected to a sense of purpose. It's love in action.

In a body, the lungs breathe in oxygen, the stomach digests food, the brain orchestrates activities, and the feet carry the body to where it should be. A healthy body doesn't have parts or organs that compete with each other or hoard resources. Can you imagine if your heart tried to compete with your lungs? They are *co-essential*. I'm coining the term here as a new word to express interdependency in the body and in a community of coworkers. Each part of the body has its own important and necessary job that supports the others. When working with others in a business, all members should work together as one organism to bring to life a shared intention. In this way, we live being of maximum use to each other.

To that end, the quest for information and the desire for growth are intrinsic motivators in both human bodies and in business. Good health in humans is associated with proper physical and psychological nourishment. A body can achieve a certain homeostasis when it is supplied with the necessities—at which point it is best equipped to be useful to others. A Human Business is much the same.

Inversely, when a body or business is diseased, it must focus on survival and has a low capacity to be useful to others. I have seen businesses become ill from toxins such as gossip, resentment, greed, and misaligned values.

A Human Business model goes beyond this analogy. It recognizes that businesses are run by humans. It acknowledges and embraces the fact that humans have strengths and weaknesses. People make mistakes. A Human Business accounts for this by creating systems and processes to cultivate a fear-free environment where everyone is safe to share, create, collaborate, and address mistakes in a supportive community.

WHY IS A HUMAN BUSINESS NEEDED?

Business can be joyful and fulfilling for people who have a common desire to serve others. Yet many traditional business philosophies prioritize making as much money as possible for the owners or stakeholders. This strategy can cause divisiveness as we compete with colleagues for promotions or recognition and battle against our competitors to sell the most products to as many customers as possible, **void of concern for what the customers actually need**. This often leads to a lower-quality product in a race to the bottom.

Another problem with the traditional approach to business is recruiting for personal expertise. Recruiting for personal expertise,

void of concern for an attitude of caring, is a recipe for competition. What happens in the workplace is that, rather than being a place of belonging, it becomes a place where people must prove themselves by outperforming their coworkers. I'm not saying that individual competency doesn't matter; it does. But competency is second to caring. Without caring, the environment becomes cold. Coldness creates a perceived separation between work life and "real" life, the life with friends and family. Work becomes time spent between the weekends. Then, if we're lucky, after forty years of dreading Mondays, we finally get to retire and never have to think about work again.

These ways of thinking and working are effective for some, but too often the result is a personal feeling of uselessness and disconnection—**a deep lack of purpose**. To bring purpose back—and to make it our top priority—I seek a different, kinder, and more holistic way of doing business.

Now that I am in my sixties, I am focusing on future plans for the company. This might look like **transitioning partial ownership to a group of interested employees**. To make this a reality, full adoption of our principles, values, and company intention is paramount. I want to pass on what I have learned through my years of experience building a different kind of business. It would be my greatest privilege to see SnapCab continue to grow and succeed.

I strive to prepare SnapCab to last far into the future, long after I'm gone. It's unrealistic to think that the company will grow and flourish based on the head knowledge of new leaders who say, "Remember how we used to do things when Glenn was around?" Just as DNA serves as a set of instructions for the functioning, growth, and flourishing of a human organism, we need a set of instructions—a Human Business model—to inform the functioning, growth, and flourishing of the company. The intention is that this book be used as a reference, a kind of constitution, for the current team as well as the next generation of SnapCab leaders. **It is only by setting up SnapCab to last as a Human Business that we can display for others how business as a whole can look different, now and in the future.** It is only by our creating a constitution for SnapCab that you can create your own constitution for your own Human Business.

Ultimately, this book is designed for the person who wants to start a business, or who is part of a business today. If you're reading this right now, you either want your own business community or have one already. As such, you may want to stop now and ask yourself, *Why am I in business? What is my definition of success?*

If you can't answer that question right away, you're not alone. In my experience, it takes deliberate self-reflection and time away from the whirlwind of daily life to allow space for insights to appear.

MY DEFINITION OF SUCCESS: A LIFE OF USE

Your definition of success determines your basic aim in life—your intention, the point from which all action flows. There is not just one definition of success. Here are a few I'm aware of: Some think that success is living as long as possible. Others, placing their hope in artificial intelligence, define success as gaining the choice to opt out of work altogether. Many business owners, set on minimizing labor costs, view success as having as few people working for the company as possible. I would like to use this book to propose a new definition of success. **Success is doing our best to live out a life of usefulness at work and help others to do the same thing**, regardless of how long or how well we do it, and expecting a continuous flow of problems for the sake of our **continuous improvement** in a community of co-essential teammates.

In other words, the paths we choose to follow in pursuit of success are the very paths that transform us and define our nature. Success need not be a singular achievement but a *continuous journey* of self-discovery and fulfillment. If our goal is to inspire others to live meaningful lives, then we all have the opportunity to grow and evolve.

Just as a human body functions best when it has lots of support—nutritious food to eat, medicine to help the healing process, and a healthy balance between physical exercise and rest—businesses, too, function best when their workers have lots of support: good equipment to work with, training and education, a kind environment in which to assess problems, and a healthy work-life balance. When individuals are well, they contribute meaningfully and, as a result, the community as a whole thrives.

HOW DOES A HUMAN BUSINESS COME ALIVE?

A Human Business is both a mindset and a business model composed of five principles that we'll discuss in further detail in the upcoming chapters. These five principles are as follows:

1. CREATE A FOUNDATION OF CARING

Cultivating kindness in the workplace builds a safe and supportive environment that unlocks the full potential of our teammates.

2. UNDERSTAND YOUR RULING LOVE

We want teammates to understand what they love to do and what gives them energy. It's important that teammates share this knowledge with leadership.

3. FOCUS ON BEING USEFUL

People are led by what they love. By working together to identify the useful target that most aligns with a teammate's ruling love, we pave the way for purpose and happiness at work.

4. EMBRACE PROBLEMS AND WEAKNESSES

Find the gold by sharing what is going wrong without blame or retribution. This transforms the workplace into a supportive community of teammates who serve each other to benefit the customer.

5. MODEL YOUR BUSINESS AFTER THE HUMAN FORM

It's a model that replaces competition with collaboration. Leadership (the head) is informed and aligned with every part of the whole (the body). We need a variety of people who can use their different loves and interests to support each other in doing something useful. One example: Your lungs are very different from your heart, but having both allows you to exist. The same is true inside your organization—you need diverse talents working in harmony.

I do not wish to take credit for these five principles. Throughout my life, I have had the great privilege of learning from mentors, other business owners, and books. It is because of this education that I was able to identify the five principles that, I believe, every Human Business should use as its foundation. And they've been tested too, right here at SnapCab. I believe they do a great job of guiding and supporting our intention of **creating communities of usefulness**.

The first four principles—create a foundation of caring, understand your ruling love, focus on being useful, and embrace problems and weaknesses—are personal; they are ways in which each of us can work on ourselves to grow as individuals while developing an orchestrated mindset for collaboration. This prepares team members to **work together as a human body**, represented by the fifth principle. This final principle is organization-focused and able to occur once the first four are openly accepted and practiced by the members of the team— including the leadership team. You'll quickly see how important it is to grow ourselves first *and strategically* so that we are then able to grow together to build a community.

I'm in a unique position because I am the owner of a business that I also view as a community. We come together for a single purpose: to be useful to others. Many people get into business solely to make money for personal gain. I have chosen to invest in building a business model that can benefit others.

A Human Business might seem like a lofty idea, a dream that could never be a reality. Gossip, resentment, greed, misaligned values, and more are common in workplaces and business in general. The Human Business isn't immune to this negativity. But with the foundation outlined in this book, and with a growing awareness of the values and principles attained from lived experience, you will gain access to support that can remain even as you fall in and out of alignment with your Human Business values, commitments, and priorities.

Yes, you will undoubtedly fall out of alignment—likely many times throughout your career. But what if I told you that falling out of alignment is necessary? Acceptance of this fact is a critical part of the Human Business philosophy: If you are unaware that the company has fallen out of alignment, how will you find your way back? This book will help you recognize where you are on your journey and realign you with your core intention, shedding old behaviors and practicing new ones as you go. Building a company—working as one body—is a continuous work in progress. It is an ongoing transformation.

WHAT ABOUT PEOPLE WHO DON'T WANT TO BE HERE?

Not everyone is on board with Human Business thinking. Some struggle with a collaborative culture, preferring instead to be consulted as the experts. These people may be driven by a desire to move up at the cost of their coworkers. Others may just want a job and desire no connection with it when they go home. Still others are only concerned with money and the grind required to get it. This book is probably not for people with those motives. This book is for employees seeking a higher purpose. It is for employers seeking to provide what Fast Company calls a raise in *emotional salary*—that is, "nonmonetary compensation that impacts how people feel about their job, like culture, career, and work-life balance."

Some people leave SnapCab to pursue new opportunities or to start their own ventures. Whenever this happens, the resignation is accepted by leadership with complete understanding. According to the Human Business philosophy, no one should spend years of their life somewhere where they do not feel aligned with their true desires. The source of this idea was my trip to Japan in 2015, during which I learned directly from Ritsuo Shingo—the former president of Toyota China and son of Dr. Shigeo Shingo, one of the architects of the Toyota Production System. Ritsuo taught me that leadership has the responsibility to not waste an employee's life.

FOSTERING DEVELOPMENT

Clear communication with employees is a top priority at SnapCab, starting with the language of a job posting in the recruitment process. It is our aim to define the type of business SnapCab is from the outset of a candidate's journey. The idea is to attract and recruit people who have a similar mindset of building a **community of usefulness**. To get a feel for who we are, check out our Careers page at SnapCab.com and keep reading to learn more about our recruitment approach in upcoming chapters.

We have a growing team of employees who are open, earnest, and interested in learning together and reaching aligned goals. Our team members may not arrive at SnapCab with the most experience or highest expertise, but **each of us has an interest in growing with the company and as people**, and **that's all that is required**. In most cases, our management team can provide the necessary training for newer members to fulfill their roles.

Each employee has their own **employee development plan** that they build in collaboration with their own manager and the company's employee experience specialist. Meeting once a year to review and update the plan ensures that both SnapCab and the individual are benefiting from the time spent together. In preparation for this discussion, employees are asked to answer questions such as What upsets you? or What things do you value and care deeply about? The plan is an effort to align what the person loves to do with what SnapCab needs to be useful to its customers. Each team member acts to meet the needs of the department that they are best suited to serve. There is a natural match between the two. Our team members love what they do each day and don't race for the door when the shift is over.

Just as the give and take between the cells of a human body creates health, giving and receiving between people creates happiness. A Human Business should make space for friendships, celebrations, workshops, and other social events designed for aligning and fostering human relationships.

Here's another thing that may surprise you: People are paid well at SnapCab. A Human Business does not trade financial security for usefulness; there is room for both. But we must get our priorities straight: usefulness first. When a useful and caring culture is the main focus, relationships flourish, trust builds, and financial abundance can increase accordingly.

IN A NUTSHELL ...

What if the secret to a wildly successful business wasn't ruthless competition but radical empathy? Human Businesses are proving that putting people first—creating supportive communities of usefulness—isn't just good ethics; it's brilliant business. Employees thrive, customers become advocates, and profit becomes a by-product of purpose. More and more books and articles have been appearing about improving the workplace, including supportive evidence that positive cultures are more productive. So, are you ready to learn more?

Create a Foundation of Caring

A caring environment is to a human soul
what warmth is to a human body.
—GLENN BOSTOCK

As a child, I struggled to tolerate my life. I will tell you all about this because it was the foundation for the life of gratitude and happiness—at work, of all places—that was to come. This Human Business model is not something I invented. It is the result of a lifetime of experiences, principles, and wisdom imparted to me by influential authors and personal mentors. Starting in childhood, I had experiences that affected my ability to enjoy my community and contribute to it. Some of these experiences were wonderful, but others were painful and were the blueprints of the lessons I was going to learn.

When I was growing up, I spent almost all of my free time with my best friend, Greg Glebe, a boy from my neighborhood. Our friendship formed the foundation of my career as a designer and manufacturer.

We had so much in common, including the fact that both of our fathers were woodworkers. My dad was a mechanical engineer and business leader by day and a hobbyist woodworker by night; Greg's dad was a craftsman. Greg and I spent hours meandering in the nearby forest and making things in our fathers' woodshops. We collected wood and metal from the local junkyard to invent gadgets and build things such as coasters, forts, rafts, and even hang gliders.

Once, we made a sail car using a sail from a boat and took it for a ride around a large parking lot.

Boats were also a big part of my childhood. While still in elementary school, I built an eight-foot boat on my own and, later, a forty-foot sailboat with my brothers and father.

I love taking raw material and building something. I learn kinetically. For Greg and me, it was play, but looking back, I think we did a lot of advanced engineering and design. We had a great time sharing a passion for working with our hands and learning from each other, and we still do to this day. Greg is the founder and owner of Xylem Design, now doing business as Pedestal Source. It makes display products for commercial and residential use. Greg and I still connect weekly to talk business, projects, and personal life.

We have always shared a mutual respect and a genuine interest in each other. We were collaborative and never competed. We trusted each other. I knew he cared about me. This friendship not only was a lifesaver at the time but also served as a foundation for my current understanding of how acceptance and support help people thrive at work.

Despite the fun and imaginative play I experienced outside of school, my experience in school was completely different.

In first grade, my teacher would add a folding screen around my desk on occasion so I could only see the blackboard instead of my classmates or the window—a tactic that made me realize I was different from my peers.

Fortunately, the students in second grade were still kind to me. But by the time I entered fourth grade at ten years old, each day was miserable. I could barely get myself to school because I dreaded everything about my day.

Shame and low self-esteem were regular feelings for me. My skin would break out into hives. At the time, I didn't recognize this as stress. When it reoccurred as an adult during a stressful episode, I made the connection.

One day, I was invited to leave the classroom with a small group of students by a woman named Jane Beebe. She helped me learn by listening rather than by reading. I was met where I was, how I was, and I began to make progress.

Later that year, I started working one-on-one with a new tutor named Donnette Alfelt. Even though we worked together at a card table inside a poorly lit boiler room, I felt warm and cared for because Donnette provided the individualized teaching I needed through kinetic games and hands-on problem-solving. These tutoring sessions helped change the trajectory of my school experience.

My fourth-grade teacher, Alison Glenn Larsen, wrote a report for my parents and future teachers so they could have a clear understanding of what she observed in class before and during my tutoring experiences. This letter highlights the many struggles, as well as small successes, I experienced that year. I didn't learn of this report until I was in my mid-forties, when my mother shared it with me. The letter changed my perception of myself and of my relationship with my mom. It helped explain my mom's low expectations for my life and her confusion about my eventual business success.

At first, I hesitated to share this letter, but it is too important to keep hidden. The letter revealed to me that the consequence of an uncaring environment is fear and suffering. The consequence of a caring, supportive environment allows my best self to surface; my enjoyment and productivity naturally flow from that place of warmth and safety.

SUMMARY REPORT ON GLENN BOSTOCK

Pupil: Glenn Bostock

Grade: Four

Year: 1970–71

Teacher: Alison G. Larsen

This report is written in an effort to help those who will be working with Glenn in the future. The first part of the report is a description of my thoughts and reactions to Glenn, as he appeared when he came to me in the fall. The second part is a description of the changes in Glenn that occurred when he began having regular steady tutoring.

Glenn's attendance was quite regular, but it was with great effort that he arrived in the morning, and he was almost always late. When he did arrive, it was all he could do to shake hands with me, mumble good morning, and put his books away. He was extremely sluggish and unresponsive. He picked up a little as the day went on, but not much. He seemed to tolerate everything and enjoy nothing. He was uninvolved with what was going on around him.

Glenn's emotions showed very little. He rarely laughed. Nor did he cry. He just sat, silent, and detached from everything that was given to him to do. When I spoke to him, he seemed not to hear. And when I repeated things, he failed to understand my meaning. He appeared to be completely uninvolved emotionally.

Glenn was equally unresponsive to his peers in the classroom. He did not participate in discussions, nor enjoy their remarks. Again, he seemed not to listen. The few times he spoke in class, it was to ask a simple question such as "What is the date?" even though the question had already been asked and the answer written on the board.

Glenn's apparent emotional tie-up kept him silent and unresponsive most of the time. Occasionally, however, with a sudden burst of feeling, he would change personality and become, for a moment, the center of attention.

This happened when he had a joke to tell or a story to relate, but never with anything directly related to school. I was glad for these occasional times when Glenn appeared relaxed and confident. At the same time, they made me aware of how Glenn was suffering under the routine of the school day. The difference between the "school Glenn" and the "joking Glenn" was so great that I could hardly believe it was the same child. For the moment that he was telling a joke, Glenn spoke beautifully—clearly, loudly, and with expression. Yet Glenn's usual voice was no more than a mumble, so low that it was difficult to understand him.

I tried every approach I could think of to motivate and interest him, but nothing seemed to achieve more than a temporary response, and even that took some doing. The minute I left Glenn's side, he would stop even trying to work, and would often begin doodling or fidgeting with some contraption in his desk. Even this behavior was done unenthusiastically.

The more complex the directions, the more frustrated Glenn became.

Written directions were even more frustrating to Glenn because of a very limited ability to read. It was simply impossible to expect him to get anything done without reading directions for him and explaining the word concepts, piece by piece.

One thing that amazed me about Glenn was his willingness to write for a creative assignment. In spite of great difficulties with spelling, when he had the opportunity, he seemed most anxious to express himself. Most often, his stories were quite mechanical and barely decipherable, but occasionally he would get his imagination into one and really enjoy it. I encouraged him all I could here and read excitedly what he wrote without marking or chastising him for his miserable form.

Although Glenn's class is one of extremes of ability, it became evident to me that Glenn's over-all ability to cope with our Fourth Grade classroom was so far below standards that he could find only greater and greater frustration by remaining in it. Seeing the contrast between the occasional imaginative and vivacious incidents and the lifeless Glenn that was tolerating everything around him with silent despair only added to my feeling that this child was being seriously harmed in the classroom. He was being subjected to work that was totally beyond him and was having the life taken out of him in the process.

Glenn's reading was at first or beginning second grade level, both his comprehension and his oral facility. A poor memory and lack of structure on which to hang things added to the difficulty of having a very limited knowledge of phonics. Glenn's reading was almost totally a hit or miss affair with the misses predominating. His ability to spell was as bad. His attempts to sound out words often resulted in combinations far removed from what he should have heard.

e.g. little = litk

Other errors resulted from some idea that there were phonic patterns, but little idea of what they were.

Somewhere along the line, Glenn appeared to have learned the doubling rule, and for a while he used it everywhere, for vowels and consonants alike.

e.g. were = weerr his = hiss

But rarely could Glenn see a pattern and apply it correctly. His background of knowledge in language was extremely limited.

In January, Jane Beebe and I met with Glenn's parents. Jane had been working with Glenn an hour or so a week, but this was not regular enough or long enough to do much good. I was convinced that the only hope for Glenn was to put him in a special school or to have someone in our school help him full-time for the skill subjects. He had been struggling for so long that he appeared to have given up and was simply ensuring what seemed to be his inevitable fate. Not only was he falling farther and farther behind, but he also seemed to be growing more and more disturbed to the extent that we wondered if there was some psychiatric problem that was deep enough to warrant help.

Fortunately, Jane Beebe saw Glenn's problems as serious enough that she was willing to take him for two hours a day of private help.

The results of this help exceed what I could have predicted. In four and a half months, Glenn has changed his whole outlook. Instead of being silent in class, he is responsive and cheerful. Instead of turning his ears off, he listened and tried to understand and accomplish. Glenn even gets to school earlier in the morning and is much less sluggish throughout the day.

Glenn has a long way to go in catching up to the class. His confidence has been down for a long time, and it can be built only gradually. But there has been steady progress in Glenn's attitudes. The psychological factors which seemed to burden him are gradually disappearing, and a cheerful, fun-loving boy is emerging. The first time Glenn talked back to me, with a twinkle in his eye, I almost cried!

> Somehow, Glenn must continue to have this intense, creative help in the skill areas. The few times he has come back to the classroom for these areas, he has tried, but has quickly sunk back into his old states of despair. Glenn has accepted this half private/half group instruction beautifully. I only hope that he can continue to have it.

I learned relatively quickly working with the tutors, and my confidence went way up. Even though I was still grades behind my classmates, between my tutor and me, I felt I was a respected person who could add value. I thought, *Wow, I really can do things!*

Despite these small successes, my parents and teachers still worried about my academic abilities. At one point, my parents considered enrolling me in more specialized schools for children with disabilities.

It wasn't until the eighth grade that we realized I had been reading cross-eyed, seeing one word as two. This made the idea of scanning a line of text seem impossible. I always felt like the stupid guy in the class. The effect of my environment on my self-esteem made it hard for me to think straight, remember things, or answer questions.

I also lived like a sugar addict. I loved sugar so much that at one point, my parents gave me a cotton candy machine. It was awesome! But I always had very low energy and headaches. Later that same year, I was diagnosed with hypoglycemia. The diagnosis explained a lot.

THE FRUIT OF FAILURE

My struggle with academics throughout my school career taught me lessons I've held on to and used throughout my life: I am very comfortable with failure, and I understand the importance of feeling cared for. When I was playing with my friend Greg or working with my tutors, I felt cared for and respected. They were interested in what I had to say, and they communicated with me at the speed and in a format I could understand.

When I felt cared for, I was willing to open up and felt my self-confidence increase, like the energy you feel on a warm, sunny spring day. **When I didn't feel cared for, I shut down**, couldn't function, and had incredible difficulty getting through the day, like the feeling of a cold, overcast winter day.

As an adult, I ran into a former schoolmate in a coffee shop. This schoolmate began asking questions about my career, family, and life. In response, I dropped my debit card and food. I was immediately uncomfortable and anxious. I reverted right back into my fourth-grade self.

My time with Greg and my tutor taught me that you change as a person depending on the company you choose to keep: Your spirit is either cared for and brought to the surface—or it isn't, so it stays below the surface.

Unfortunately, my experience isn't uncommon. Everyone has a story. Some of us try to close the door to the chapter in our lives that brought us pain. But all of our experiences have a lesson, and it can be useful to share our lessons to benefit others.

Today, my awareness of the need to build a foundation of caring at SnapCab is at the forefront of the company's activities. I understand that a person can thrive when they feel cared for.

In contrast, a person's potential is stunted when they feel the absence of care. For example, SnapCab team members are not encouraged to compare themselves to each other because it is an unsupportive practice that can turn friends and teammates into competitors.

Now that I'm in the position to build and lead an organization, I want to make sure people feel comfortable. **A foundation of caring must come first; otherwise, people won't feel comfortable being themselves.**

A focus on caring first is something I continue to work on every day. A Human Business acknowledges that we all make mistakes: At times, I have transferred my frustration onto others. When I do fail to put caring first, it is my aim to recognize it and apologize, since my frustration is not others' problem.

HOW SNAPCAB CREATES A FOUNDATION OF CARING

At SnapCab, we are continually building systems that offer people the opportunity to feel cared for. Once a year, each team member gets a tailor-made **anniversary video**. This short video—only a few minutes long—is produced by the employee's manager and features testimonials from their colleagues. The video covers how the team member demonstrates company values, and it includes an overview of their job and the qualities they bring to the community and provides a glimpse into family life or personal hobbies. Once finished, the video is broadcast to the entire company, so everyone can participate in congratulating the person for their achievements.

What's so beautiful about this gift is that it gives those who work closely with the celebrated team member an opportunity to express appreciation for that person's contributions; and it gives the entire community a small window into the team member's life at work and at home. This is one of my favorite caring tools at SnapCab because so often people go through life without being acknowledged. This system warmly recognizes each and every employee in a public way.

Another initiative serves up company-wide welcome breakfasts for new hires in their first month of work. The SnapCab team also sends meals and flowers to team members who are celebrating big life events or experiencing difficult times. In fact, when the whole team hit hard times in March of 2020, it was the mutual care of SnapCab team members that got many of us through the uncertainty of the pandemic. The focus was, at first, a paralyzing fear for health, safety, and livelihood. But when the SnapCab leadership team channeled energy into expressing care for our team members—checking in with each person by phone and arranging for the delivery of diapers and groceries—we found our relationships strengthened.

These caring practices aren't revolutionary; the key is to build them into company systems so that they aren't merely a part of head knowledge but rather a part of a documented system that prompts our caring practices to happen automatically.

Understand Your Ruling Love

The only way to do great work is to love what you do.
—STEVE JOBS

Throughout adolescence and early adulthood, my love for woodworking grew along with me. Despite difficulties in most school subjects, this was an area where I excelled and found genuine joy. I spent much of my free time perfecting the craft, losing myself in the rhythm of creating something beautiful and functional with my hands.

Following high school, I attended Bucks County Community College and majored in fine woodworking. For once, I enjoyed my courses: woodshop, woodworking history, pottery, glassblowing, and creative problem-solving. I dreamed of becoming a famous craftsman who designed, built, and sold original furniture through galleries. I was motivated by the freedom of building whatever I wanted.

This experience taught me something crucial that would later become foundational to how I hire and develop employees: When people do what they love, they don't watch the clock. They lose themselves in the work. Time moves differently when you're engaged in something that energizes rather than drains you. This was my first glimpse into what I now call a person's "ruling love."

I would often visit furniture galleries to study the work of masters. One such visit was especially informative. In 1981, I saw a piece made by Wharton Esherick, the father of modern woodworking. I was excited and in awe. I approached the piece and marveled at the craftsmanship and beauty. Then I noticed the price tag: $2,000! I would expect an impressive piece like that to cost closer to $15,000, even if it was made by an unknown like me, and much more if made by one of the masters. After seeing it being sold for such a low price, I realized there was no way I was going to make a living doing this type of work.

Even though I was disappointed by this market reality, I had such a love for building one-of-a-kind furniture that I decided to focus my career plans on providing high-end custom cabinetry and furniture for clients. This pivot taught me an important lesson: Sometimes we must adapt the expression of our love while staying true to its essence.

A ruling love is a deep, inexplicable desire to do one thing that lights you up, brings you joy, and allows you to experience a flow state where time seems to race by. Your ruling love is the reason you want to get up in the morning; it motivates you to do the things you do each day.

Each of us has a ruling love that drives us in life, and if possible, we build our life through **subordinate loves** that support us in fulfilling our ruling love. Maybe what you love most in life is the sense of freedom you experience while motorbiking. You'll likely build your life around fulfilling that love every chance you get. You'll spend your time purchasing, riding, and maintaining your bike. You'll participate in events with other people who enjoy the sport. Each of these activities is a **supporting love** that helps you fulfill your ruling love of freedom through motorbiking.

If your ruling love is self-expression through painting, you may go to art stores, purchase and organize supplies, visit art galleries, or take drawing classes. Each of these activities is a supporting love that helps you fulfill your ruling love of self-expression through painting.

Even down to the coffee you drink, the food you eat, the clothes you wear, the home you live in, and the person you marry, all may be chosen to support your ruling love. Take a moment to consider that.

If you are unable to make space for your ruling love, you may feel depleted, agitated, and dissatisfied. You may suspect that you are not living life to its full potential. Ultimately, your days amount to a growing pile of resentments for mundane activities, responsibilities, and people. Can you identify with this version of living?

FROM ME TO WE

I made some great friends in college, one of whom was Steve Metz. What brought us together was a shared admiration for the same two influential woodworkers. We both respected the clean, simple, and functional woodwork of James Krenov, author of *A Cabinetmaker's Notebook* and founder of the College of the Redwoods. We also loved the work of Sam Maloof, one of America's best-known contemporary furniture craftsmen.

After our first year of college, Steve and I made our way up to Canada for summer employment. We had two jobs lined up: One included building a kitchen and doing cabinet work at my parents' cottage on Wolfe Island, Ontario, and another included constructing a cottage at a lodge just north of Toronto in Muskoka. Little did I know what life transformation would occur at that lodge.

One hot afternoon, when I was up on the roof hammering shingles, I looked down and noticed a car approaching. Two women emerged, and one in particular caught my attention. *Who is she?* I remember thinking.

Over the summer, Cheryl and I got to know each other. The first time we were alone together, I let Cheryl drive my old Fiat because she wanted to try her hand at driving a manual car. At one point, when we were both looking at the gear shift knob, the road turned, but the car did not.

Cheryl, the Fiat, and I slowly, gracefully turned upside down into a ditch. My car door was pinned shut, but I was able to kick Cheryl's door open so the two of us could climb out and walk to the road to find help.

Fortunately, no one was hurt except for the Fiat, but I wasn't upset; I told Cheryl that I wanted a pickup truck anyway. This would be a pivotal moment in our relationship because I kept my calm and didn't get mad at Cheryl for totaling my car, a move that won her over. I was smitten too: She was a kind person who loved animals and art. We cared about each other.

At the end of the summer, when I was paid for my work at the lodge, I was given fifty dollars more than I had charged. They didn't have to do that! Receiving that extra money without expecting it was such a surprise; it left an impression on me. It was a true act of kindness. I knew that in the future I wanted to do the same for others.

This experience taught me something about generosity and care that would later inform how I treated employees: When you give people more than they expect, you create loyalty and connection that go far beyond any contractual obligation.

BECOMING A BUSINESS OWNER

When I was twenty-three, I decided to go into business for myself. I had been working for a low wage and had learned a lot by developing my skills with Dirk Odhner, a top craftsman in the area.

Cheryl and I rented a portion of a barn with two of my college friends, one being Steve. The barn had a dirt floor and a low ceiling. I had to build a floor for my workspace, so the ceiling was even lower after that. For many woodworking projects, I wouldn't see the finished piece upright until it was in the customer's house.

For sixty dollars per month, including electricity, Cheryl and I had our very own shop for our very own work. Each day, Cheryl, our dog Spike, and I would go to the barn and enjoy doing projects as a team. It was a lot of fun, and I couldn't have done it without her.

Since Cheryl and I got together so young, we really finished growing up together. I went from being dependent to independent. We got married, and I started my own business. I became my own person, the captain of my own ship. Running my own business transformed my self-image in ways I couldn't have anticipated.

I can't overstate the impact of finally feeling pride in knowing I was good at something: woodworking. I loved going to my shop, meeting with customers, designing custom pieces, working on projects, and installing high-end cabinetry and furniture. I loved being able to do every part of the job, and, admittedly, what I loved most was being able to show off my talent by doing something special that not everyone could do.

I didn't excel in school, but I excelled at woodwork. It was a skill I had that I could use. I would lose track of time, work all day, and take pride in each piece I built. It made me feel good to produce something that someone else wanted to buy.

I look back on this time with affection because I experienced immense joy living my life in a way that helped me to express my **ruling love**. The concept of a ruling love is something I learned about much later in life from my mentors, but I realize now how important it is to understand the concept as early on as possible.

LOVE, BUSINESS, AND LEARNING

In an ideal world, our professional life supports our ruling love. In reality, sometimes there is pressure to pursue a career that is seen as responsible, sensible, or lucrative, so we choose the thing we are supposed to do instead of the thing we want to do. Fears and realities about financial stability, supporting a family, or how others perceive us come into play. Our ruling love gets pushed aside, and free time turns into distractions, misusing substances, or other forms of escapism as we try to cope with the suffering that comes from an unfulfilled life.

Sometimes we are unable to focus on our ruling love because we're more focused on having our basic, foundational needs met. If we don't have enough food, water, clean air, or shelter, we are not going to be able to focus on anything else. Once basic needs are satisfied, and we have the capacity to nurture our ruling love, we can start thinking on a higher plane. We can pursue the one thing that gives us a real sense of joy in life.

Maybe you are not able to identify your ruling love at this moment. **Perhaps all you know is that you want to contribute to something bigger than yourself.** Do not underestimate this quiet seed; you are most of the way there. If this sounds like you, then perhaps your ruling love includes a sense of *caring*. If so, you are the kind of person who could find belonging in a Human Business.

I understand that not all work tasks are enjoyable or match someone's ruling love. I met with a manager of employees in the food industry who have mundane jobs. He faced an unhappy workforce and high turnover. I tried to encourage him by saying that the best he could do is to create a workplace with clear values and a culture of respect where people feel they matter and their voices are heard. In that kind of environment, someone's love of people or camaraderie can be the key. They may not enjoy the tasks themselves, but they'll do them because they love being a part of the workplace community. The work becomes subordinate to their ruling love of belonging or purpose. Your company may even be offering something that people are not finding in their own family or neighborhood. Employees themselves can meet you halfway by doing their best in their job and being part of a positive work culture. The culture isn't handed to them. It's co-created by them. They are co-essential.

While I am grateful that my wife has supported me in pursuing my ruling love in the past, and continues to do so to this day, it brings me so much joy to see Cheryl fulfill her ruling love of taking care of other living beings. She dedicates much of her time to family, especially her grandchildren. She has also returned to working with animals. In recent years, she has funneled her energy into dog training, riding horses, and tending to her chickens. When it comes to her ruling love of caring for her grandchildren, Cheryl has many supporting loves. She enjoys researching educational toys and setting up kids' spaces in our home. She is a great example of someone who has a clear ruling love. She does many things to support that love and channels them into doing something useful.

The time early in our marriage when we worked in the woodshop together is one of my favorite memories. But woodworking was not Cheryl's dream. She got a job as a veterinary technician and actually started making more money than me. I felt threatened because I wanted to be the breadwinner. I even started downplaying her success. My handling of things during this period is one of my biggest regrets. I didn't respect her career goals because I was preoccupied with what I wanted. Cheryl left her job when we started a family, and she was exceptional at raising the children. Today, we recognize that things turned out well for our family, but I do regret not having supported her more at that time.

It's not rocket science. It's important to know what you love, what you know, and what you do. But the importance is where to put the emphasis. Being aware of what you love to do is more important than knowing how to do it. And, once you learn how to do it, going and *actually doing* it is the most important thing.

ARE ALL LOVES THE SAME?

Unfortunately, our ruling love is not always a positive thing. There are tyrants in this world who have a ruling love of torturing people. There are also people who have a love of making themselves powerful. I've heard some people say that love is all that matters, but it really depends on the type of love: Is it a love of inflating our self-image, a love of gaining material things, or a love of doing what helps others?

Let's compare two politicians with the same job. They are both charged with the responsibility of addressing the effects of climate change, but they carry different types of motivation. One is ruled by a love of gaining power and fame, while the other is ruled by a love of preserving the planet for the sake of the people who live on it. Same job, different intentions. Same actions, different heart.

Organized religion tends to organize human beings into communities according to common beliefs. But I want to build a culture using a Human Business model that invites people into community according to a common love—a common heart.

This is why at SnapCab, when we're looking for new team members, we focus not just on what people love to do but on whether their love includes caring for others. We want to attract people whose ruling love drives them to be useful to their colleagues and customers.

CAN A RULING LOVE CHANGE?

Over the years, the *expression* of my ruling love has changed several times. It started with building custom fine furniture. What rules me now, forty years later, is the creativity of building communities. Each day, I receive a fresh supply of energy to work with my team to develop simple, scalable systems at SnapCab for the benefit of our customers and each other. That may seem like a big jump, but the many smaller changes that occurred over the years allowed me to realize this new motivation.

I am not the only one whose ruling love has been through a growing process. All who work for SnapCab have the opportunity to observe the growth and development of what they care about. In fact, our recruitment system and hiring process take into account what people like to do, what they want to do, and how they see themselves spending their lives. We want people to *want* to do what they're being hired to do. Once an employee has been with us for several months, we offer them an employee development meeting. In this meeting, the manager highlights the needs of the company and asks the employee what their hopes are for the next chapter of their career at SnapCab. The ideal outcome of the meeting is harmony between what the employee wants to do and what needs to be done for the good of the company. As long as care for your work and care for other people remain intact, a shift in duties can only lead to growth. Another way to say it: **As long as your ruling love includes an intention to benefit others, we will find a good means of expression for the love and skills that are unique to you.**

You may be thirsty for a change. What if you are doing your job because it's the one you've had for ten years? Or because it's good money? Maybe what you'd really like is to work because you want to. The gap between what motivates you today and what you *want* to be motivated by could be big. But observing your budding desire might be sufficient progress for today.

Your ruling love will evolve if you take one step in a new direction on a regular basis. In my case, I did not always set out to make change; rather, the opportunities to change presented themselves to me. I did not seek out a fork in the road, but a fork in the road came into view. My ruling love evolved over time with each opportunity to make a new choice.

THE BRIDGE TO USEFULNESS

I can see in retrospect that I was motivated to shift from a small life to a bigger one by both high market demand and the accompanying awareness of the opportunity for me to change on the inside. My love of woodworking was only a stepping stone. I was, at this point, invited to focus less on my narrow world and more on the bigger world of **useful service to other human beings**—a principle we'll talk about in full detail in the following chapter.

The evolution from focusing solely on my own creative expression to helping others find theirs represents a fundamental shift that every leader in a Human Business must make. It's the difference between asking "What do I love?" and asking "How can what I love serve others?"

Understanding your ruling love provides the energy and motivation for meaningful work, but it's only the beginning. The next step is learning how to channel that energy toward something larger than yourself—toward being genuinely useful to others. Because while personal passion can sustain you for a while, only usefulness can create lasting fulfillment and sustainable success.

Focus on Being Useful

Life's most persistent and urgent question is,
What are you doing for others?
—MARTIN LUTHER KING, JR.

REALIZING IT'S NOT JUST ABOUT ME

Despite being clear on my first love of building custom fine furniture, it wasn't too long before I started running into some significant challenges.

After a few years in business, Cheryl and I were struggling to make enough money to meet our basic needs. People seemed impressed by my work, but they weren't willing to pay what it was worth. The gap between admiration and actual sales was becoming a chasm I couldn't bridge.

In hindsight, I can clearly see why there were challenges. What I loved about our marriage was that Cheryl loved me. I loved being loved. Cheryl was supportive, and she made it so I could go do my work. I see now that I was focused on what I alone was getting out of the marriage.

There was a parallel in my business as well. I loved making beautiful things and loved that my customers admired what I was doing, even though my work was labor-intensive and financially unviable. No one was willing to pay me more than they were already paying for the work I was doing, so I couldn't afford to support the kids we were about to start having.

This realization hit me hard: **Having passion for your work isn't enough if that work doesn't serve a real need in the world.** I was creating beautiful furniture that impressed people, but I wasn't solving problems that they were willing to pay to have solved.

WHEN LIFE FORCES A PIVOT

After Cheryl and I were married, we decided to wait five years before starting a family to feel more established in business and adulthood. When I was twenty-seven and Cheryl was twenty-four, we became pregnant with our first child, Anne.

Cheryl experienced a normal pregnancy, and we prepared over a period of months to become a family of three. But the night before Anne was born, Cheryl realized the baby had stopped moving. She called her doctor, who told her not to worry.

The next day, when Cheryl went into labor, we went to the hospital, where she delivered a beautiful, brown-haired baby girl.

But Anne was stillborn.

It was devastating. It's a thing that shakes you up as a person. At first, I was in shock and denial. I called family and friends and told them that the birth was not happening; they were confused and didn't understand what I was saying. I couldn't find the words to say that our baby had died.

Up until that point in our lives, both Cheryl and I had looked to other people—to the adults—for help and guidance in understanding how to live life. We asked others how to buy houses or get jobs. We wanted to know how to handle this terrible situation, but no one had an answer. There was no guidebook on how to navigate losing your first child.

We grew up substantially from this experience. We became adults. Throughout the pregnancy, we hadn't made enough money to afford to buy a house, so we moved in with my grandmother, who needed help. During the day, she had healthcare workers visiting her home and providing care, and in the evening, we took over and cared for her. This situation provided a mutual benefit—we could provide needed care for my grandmother while also saving money for a down payment on a house.

But when we lost Anne, we were devastated and felt like our lives had stalled. We lost our capacity to care for my grandmother. To our relief, my Aunt Ruth, a widow who lived alone, invited us to move in with her. She offered us immense support, along with a place to begin healing. We are so grateful for her care during that difficult time in our lives. We lived with her for several months and then felt a deep urgency to find our own home, our very own place to start our family.

This experience taught me something profound about purpose and usefulness: When we're focused only on our own desires and comfort, we're unprepared for life's real challenges. We had been living in a bubble where my passion for woodworking was enough, where being loved and admired was sufficient. But real life demanded something more—it demanded resilience, service to others, and the ability to find meaning, even in suffering.

FINDING HELP AND LEARNING ABOUT TRUST

Cheryl found a house for sale in the newspaper, but we still couldn't afford the down payment. I decided to reach out for help. I chose to approach Chris Chandor, a local businessman who owned a property development company that I had worked for in the past. I really liked Chris, but I was somewhat intimidated by him. He was outgoing, successful, and a professional lawyer. But we did have a good rapport. He had been happy with the woodwork I provided in the past, including ventilation louvers for the top exterior of his office buildings, as well as custom cabinetry for the interior offices. He decided to hire me once more, but this time for a much bigger job.

Chris was in the midst of building a new house and needed extensive interior woodwork. When I shared that my wife and I were trying to buy a house, Chris responded with great generosity. He offered to buy the house that we were interested in and rent it to us, with the promise to then sell it to us once we could afford the down payment. Chris's generosity showed me that when you focus on being genuinely helpful to others, they often want to help you in return.

During one meeting with Chris, I learned the value of taking action in the present moment. He made several phone calls and recruited help from his team so that, just ten days later, Cheryl and I could move into the house. This taught me that if I can do it at all, I can do it now. I don't even have to wait to act until the meeting is over. A to-do list is not always necessary and can actually take up more time. (See the book *Getting Things Done: The Art of Stress-Free Productivity* by David Allen for more on this topic.)

Chris's property was stunning. It featured a pond and a beautiful home that I worked on for more than a year. I built multiple wall units, curved doorways with raised paneling, libraries, mantelpieces, an oak bar, a study, and a front door. I also designed and built a curved frame-and-panel wall below a stairway, a project that was featured in *Fine Homebuilding* magazine.

With Chris's direction, I tracked my time and materials and billed him after I finished each job. But in the process of doing so, I became curious about something.

One day, I was chatting with Chris and asked, "How do you know I'm giving you an accurate bill? I could be writing down any number of hours, but you never check to make sure they are correct." His answer was something I will never forget. He said that when he starts working with someone, he decides whether or not to trust them; from the beginning, he decided to trust me. Because of that trust, he paid whatever bill I gave him.

I was wowed. I deeply appreciated the trust he gave to me. Early on in my cabinet work, I would check bills very carefully to ensure that I received the right materials or that my employees were logging their exact hours. A lot of energy and anxiety went into checking to see if I was being treated fairly.

When I maintain mutual trust with the people around me, life is more relaxing, freeing all parties to channel energy into what is most useful—what is mutually beneficial. Simply put, trust and usefulness are interconnected.

Chris's approach made a lot of sense, and I have implemented it at SnapCab. That said, how do you know if people are trustworthy? To answer this, I would ask you to consider: Do you have people in your life who work to ensure they are building a relationship with you? Are there others who seem more interested in coming out on top, leaving you with the short end of the stick? Your answers may reveal the status of mutual trust in your relationships.

This lesson would later become fundamental to how I run SnapCab. When you hire people whose values align with yours, you can focus on serving customers instead of policing employees.

HARD TIMES TO TRANSFORMATION

After Cheryl and I moved into our new home, our second daughter, Carla, was born. Two years after that, we welcomed our third daughter, Rorri.

While growing our family was a priority, our family was growing faster than our income. We decided to wait to have more children. But somehow, someway, we ended up pregnant with our fourth child, Greg.

A very pregnant Cheryl was supplementing our income by making wedding cakes and hand-dipped candles at home. She enjoyed this work, but it was difficult to do the work while at home with the kids.

I felt fortunate to do the work I loved to do each day, but we could barely afford food. Cheryl would sometimes cry in the grocery store from the stress of spending money we didn't have. Finally, after years of resisting the use of public assistance, I set my pride aside, and we applied for the government's WIC program, an initiative that supported women, infants, and children. Today, I sometimes jokingly refer to WIC as a program for women, infants, and cabinetmakers.

I was stressed, tired, confused, and disappointed as to why it was so hard for me to make a living doing the thing I was gifted at. I was working hard, spending long hours in the woodshop, and borrowing money to get things off the ground.

From 1989 to 1994, the country was in a recession, and I had very little work. I could barely afford the insurance my company needed to stay in business. I fell deep into debt because I couldn't afford to pay my taxes for years. I borrowed money to help market my business for jobs but didn't see the results of that marketing until well after Greg was born. I hired Beth McGinnis to be my bookkeeper and asked her to set aside 10 percent of the company's earnings for tax repayment.

We should have gone bankrupt, but with Beth's help, we were able to dig our way out of that deep hole. It took six years to pay off the debt. Love alone won't sustain you or the people who depend on you. I needed to find a way to use my skills in service of something the world was actually asking for.

TRANSFORMING LOVE INTO USEFULNESS

The hard times had certainly laid the foundation for the better times. In 1990, my father was a partner at an elevator maintenance business in northern New Jersey. He and his partner would perform the maintenance, part of which involved fixing the interiors of elevators. What they did was scrap the shell of the elevator down to the platform and order a new shell from the factory. It was a big, expensive, laborious process, and my dad encouraged me to find a better solution.

"Hey, Glenn," he said, "there's a real need for someone to remodel elevators instead of replacing the entire thing." I considered it and realized that it might be something I could do, since an elevator interior was basically an inside-out cabinet. My dad then taught me some elevator safety essentials, including how to open the hall doors and climb on top of a cab to turn it off.

While I thoroughly enjoyed designing and building a custom project that required my individual expertise, this job opened my eyes to something new: market need. I saw an unmet need in a specific market, and I saw the potential of my business to meet it. Maybe I could use the resources of my business to serve elevator maintenance companies and their customers (the market) with a new way to update elevator interiors (the need).

Once I finished that first renovation job, I showed my full portfolio to several elevator maintenance companies in the Philadelphia area, including United Elevator, Vigil Elevator, and Penn Elevator Company. I asked if I could provide them with remodeling services, and each company responded with an enthusiastic and resounding "Yes!"

I started remodeling about one elevator interior every two months, between my other custom furniture jobs. By 1992, I was completing one elevator interior every month, and by the time Greg was born in 1994, I was completing one per week. My phone was starting to ring again.

It wasn't long after that when I hired Jason King to take on the sales role. Jason would bid on each job, and I would build and install it. When I hired Jason, the company's finances were so tight that he worked out of my living room and basement, among the kids and their toys, for over a year.

By 1998, I had stopped all other work besides elevator interior remodeling. My last cabinetry job was building a corner cabinet for the historic Bryn Athyn Cathedral in Bryn Athyn, Pennsylvania.

I had steady work. This was a first! I would spend Monday, Tuesday, and Wednesday building the elevator interior and Thursday and Friday installing it.

One client in Atlantic City stopped me mid-installation, surprised that I was the same person who had sold him the product a few weeks earlier. He asked, "Hey, aren't you the same guy—the sales guy in the suit?"

"Yes!" I said. "I am. I sell it, design it, build it, and install it."

He was amazed that one person could do all of that. But for me, it made perfect sense. I loved the work because I could see the entire process from start to finish, and I knew I was solving a real problem for real people.

THE SHIFT FROM PASSION TO PURPOSE

The transition from custom furniture to elevator remodeling taught me the difference between following your passion and being useful. When I was making custom furniture, I was following my passion but not necessarily meeting a market need. When I shifted to elevator remodeling, I found a way to use my skills to solve real problems for real people.

What the market was asking for was elevator interior remodeling, and I chose to respond to the opportunity. I didn't love the work like I loved cabinetmaking, but I realized it was much more useful work. In other words, it was mutually beneficial work. I was able to help more people, and I was also able to support my family.

It's important to highlight that my interest in useful work did not stem from virtue. In other words, it wasn't because I was good that I turned my attention to something higher than myself. On the contrary, it was when my own situation was not working anymore that I was open to considering work that was more service oriented. The fun woodworking jobs could not support my family. The less fun elevator remodeling work *did* pay because there was demand; and I could then make ends meet. I became more useful doing good work for customers because I was compelled by the needs of my family to do something different. Ultimately, my attention to my own benefit is a reminder to me that I'm not the originator of good. Instead, good—or love—uses my self-interest to consider the greater good. **Focusing on being useful has caring at its core.**

Before my business entered this new phase of development, most people couldn't figure out what I could offer—because I could offer basically anything: kitchens, bookcases, beds, rocking chairs, and sound recording studios. Through my business transition, I saw that specialization was the key to what allowed people to gain a very clear understanding of what my business offered. No longer was I a woodworker making anything for anyone. Now I was a creator of elevator interiors, making a specific product for the specific customers in need of my particular function.

A perfect image of specialization appears in the human body. Just as a stem cell divides to create muscle cells ready to help the body move, my function in the business community started as all-purpose before it became special-purpose—of special use to a particular region of the business community.

A second awareness that came of this business transition was about reaching my customers. I saw that I needed to know who my customers were and provide them with exactly what they needed; but I *also* had to have a **channel** to get to them. I identified that elevator mechanics were the customers I needed to focus on, as they were the ones who were working with my product in order to make *their* customers happy—the building owners. The elevator maintenance companies were the channel through which I could get to my customers. In custom cabinetwork, I had no sales channel and, therefore, no obvious path to the next job. But now I had a place to go—a place to *return* to—with predictability. My company and elevator maintenance companies shared a common end user—the building owners. This made elevator maintenance companies a great channel to a continuous source of jobs via an ongoing flow of potential customers—their mechanics. If we can provide these mechanics with what they need to install an elevator interior with ease and efficiency, we are doing our part to serve the end user as well. At SnapCab, we focus on the mechanics. If we can equip them to install interiors efficiently, we can serve building owners anywhere in the world.

Making the choice to commit myself, my attention, and my business to elevator interior remodeling required me to sacrifice one expression of my love of woodworking. But it wasn't gone; it just took new form. I found a way to use my ruling love of woodworking to address customer demand. In other words, **I combined what I love to do with what is useful**. This is still the approach to my work that I use now, more than twenty-five years after I first embraced it.

A LESSON IN PRIORITIES

I admit that when I was a young adult, I was very focused on fulfilling my own wants, something I believe many people experience in their youth. When I was a kid, my brothers and I would walk three miles round-trip to the Marysville corner store on Wolfe Island in the hopes of getting our hands on some ice cream. We would collect pop bottles along the way for their five-cent return. If we found enough bottles, we could get enough money back to buy an ice cream cone. Our focus was getting ice cream; collecting recycled bottles and helping the planet was merely a by-product. As I got older, I made a conscious decision to do more useful things, just because it's the right thing to do.

I had another experience in childhood that helped hone my understanding of usefulness. As a young adult, I went on a ski trip with my brothers. Since we had little money, we rented skis and dressed in mechanic jumpsuits instead of proper snow gear. Despite having a wonderful experience on the slopes, I decided not to pursue skiing. I could either spend my time and money on skiing or spend that time woodworking—something that could lead to a career. I made a choice to forgo entertainment in favor of pursuing woodworking as a practical investment. This investment has grown into a multimillion-dollar company. I had limited resources; I had to be selective about how I used them.

I'm not implying that people shouldn't pursue activities they enjoy or only choose activities that make money. I love to boat and, now that I can afford to do it, I boat to recharge and refresh my mind so that I can go and fulfill my purpose. That said, if you can align your ruling love with something that is useful to someone else, you can live a very fulfilled life, one that surprises you in the best of ways. Good things will start to flow to you, and you'll be astonished by how everything falls into place. You'll get exactly what you need when you need it, as if there were some unseen force magically orchestrating the events leading to your success. You'll start to feel greater joy with the fulfillment of working toward something higher, and you'll likely make more than enough money to go and do it.

MONEY, MENTORSHIP, AND DETERMINING WHAT'S USEFUL

By now, you know that moneymaking is not my first priority in business. But it can be an indicator of usefulness. A business must be sustainable to ensure its ongoing usefulness in the communities it serves. That observation seems obvious now, but it eluded me at the outset of my career. Only through mentorship did I access a new perspective on the role of profitmaking in business.

Let me explain. Through my small-town community in Pennsylvania, I discovered a group of three retired businessmen who offered free mentorship to local business owners. As members of ABG Consulting, Ed Asplundh (retired president of Asplundh Tree Expert Co.), Dick Brickman (retired owner of The Brickman Group), and Howard Gurney (a financial expert and banker) took me under their wing to share what had brought each of them success in business. My company benefited immediately from the guidance I received.

I remember one conversation in particular. I showed them my portfolio of custom cabinetwork and got candid about my intention: I wasn't trying to make abundant amounts of money, I told them. But Dick responded, "You know, Glenn, money isn't all bad; it's what you do with the money that makes all the difference. A school wouldn't have books if someone didn't make money and donate the books to the school."

Dick's response helped me see that, if used intentionally, money is fuel to do good. You can use it to donate books to a school, and you can use it to keep a useful business going. Making money can be good.

In addition to offering a new perspective on money in business, my mentors helped me with other business decisions. I trusted them to guide my choices at a critical time in the company. So, when they encouraged me to continue to focus on elevator interior remodeling, I took it as a sign that my internal compass was worth following, and I could make the decision to shift my focus completely. That was the end of my woodworking business and the beginning of my elevator interior business.

I soon invented a new way of remodeling elevators: a kit of parts. The kit featured a horizontal interlocking paneling (ILP) system that had several advantages over traditional vertical hanging panels. Dick encouraged me to patent it, which I did. The whole system was easy to order, easy to manufacture, and easy to install. So easy, in fact, that elevator mechanics could install it with no prior experience. This was a boon to the elevator industry.

WHAT MAKES SOMETHING USEFUL?

Through this experience, I learned that usefulness is a combination of three essential elements: love, knowledge, and action.

- **Love:** You need to want to do it, have a desire to do it, and be motivated to do it. *You need to care about it.*
- **Knowledge:** You need to know how to do it, know the truth about it, or understand the means by which you intend to do it.
- **Action:** You need to go do it. This last element is key. Without an action plan, the desire to do something and the means to do it will never be enough to bring a proposal to life. **If it's not actionable, it's of no use.**

THE SNAPCAB BRAND: USEFULNESS IN ACTION

It has been my aim so far in this book to convey that the SnapCab name comes down to one word. Who we are, what we care about, and our purpose for being in business is *usefulness*. In every decision we make and in every interaction we have, we seek to do what is useful—that is, what is helpful. We seek to be of service to each **customer**, whether that customer is a coworker, a vendor, or someone who wants to buy our custom privacy pods. When presented with a project proposal, we ask ourselves one simple question: Is it useful? If the answer is yes, the project is worth our consideration.

COMPANY VALUES REFLECT OUR AIM TO BE OF USE

The way we remember to follow the recipe for usefulness is by consulting our company values (be kind, be authentic, and be useful), each of which is rooted in the aforementioned elements.

- **Be kind:** Love comes first. Practicing kindness places emphasis on connection over competition. It is more important to *care* about each other (and about a project) than it is to evaluate each other based on how much each person knows.

- **Be authentic:** We all have unique strengths and weaknesses. Sharing them fosters understanding and collaboration, turning weaknesses into opportunities for others to help. Authenticity thrives in a kind environment.

- **Be useful:** Usefulness comes last, not because it's the least important, but because usefulness comes to life in actions only when it's based on kindness and authenticity.

Using simple values to guide our decision-making is, in itself, a useful practice. Outside of business, we might rely on beliefs, politics, or religion to filter our decision-making. But using universal values to help filter project priorities allows us to maintain unity of purpose at work.

How do we bring these values to life? It's simple: We create order. We build systems and processes for everything we do, from big projects to the everyday. If we think of a business as a human body, then creating order happens in every single part—from the foundational skeleton to each tiny, individual cell. Every system is carefully orchestrated and designed to create order. This isn't just about showing up on time (though that's part of it!). It's about creating a structure that makes it easy for us to be genuinely kind and authentic. When we're organized and efficient, we have the tools and the clarity to make a real difference. That means having clear standard operating procedures (SOPs) for all the good we do, so we can focus on what matters most: doing something that is useful.

It is my hope, reader, that you will **adopt this simple set of values** to guide your **caring, thinking, and acting** in your own community!

LOVE LEADS TO LEARNING

So far, we've covered my own story of aligning my ruling love with usefulness. In other words, we've covered love and use. But we have yet to cover knowledge. I have deliberately omitted discussion of knowledge until now. Why? In the business world, there seems to be a hyperfocus on knowledge. Of course, it's important to go to school and learn, but sometimes it seems like education and expertise are the only things that are considered valuable. My own experience has shown me that culture shifts when people in a workplace rank themselves based on knowledge alone. The environment becomes toxic with ill will, competition, and a shared focus on results instead of purpose.

Here's what I know: Knowledge can be gained. If I want to do something, I can learn how to do it. But if I lack the motivation to do something, it doesn't really matter what I know; it won't be done well, period. Now let's talk about you, a leader in your community. If you decide to teach one of your employees how to do something that they do not care about, you may be delaying the happiness of all parties. I am talking about the happiness that can be realized when an employee's particular love is paired with a particular need of the greater community. If your employee cannot yet fulfill the need because of a lack of knowledge, they can acquire what they need to know—if they want to know it. Love leads to learning.

RECRUITMENT: A FILTER FOR LOVE, NOT EXPERTISE

If usefulness begins with love, then recruitment should start there too. At SnapCab, instead of hiring employees based on their credentials, we hire based on desire. We like hiring people who are excited to join the SnapCab team and are energized to learn. We favor these applicants over those who boast an impressive résumé but lack the desire to apply their ruling love to serve the needs of the whole.

Since revamping SnapCab's recruitment system to attract compatible candidates, an interesting phenomenon has emerged during interviews. Many candidates are open to taking on any role, as long as there's an opportunity to join the team. A candidate once said to me, "I don't even care if what you're saying in the videos on your website is fully happening. If your intention is there, that's all that matters to me."

Here's one story along those lines: Tim had learned from Micah, a friend working at SnapCab, what the company was all about. So Tim applied for a position as a project manager. During the interview process, it became clear that Tim had many years of experience in the world of marketing. "Why did you apply for project management?" I asked Tim.

"I want to work here," he said, "and that is the job that is open."

I was impressed by his desire to be part of the SnapCab community but did not hire him for that position. Instead, recognizing that communications was one of his loves, I invited him to be part of our marketing team. Tim has been a wonderful addition to the community ever since and currently contributes as our marketing manager for the US location in Warrington, Pennsylvania.

In a nutshell: First, we bring you aboard. Then we consider your role. Who you are is what matters the most. **If who you are includes a love of caring, you belong here from the get-go.**

THE IMPACT OF USEFULNESS

When I decided to aim my love of woodworking at something useful, my business grew. The decision to use my woodworking skills to meet an existing market need led to an extraordinary market response. That's how we knew the customers were happy.

The word *customer* did not just apply to the end users—the building owner and the person inside the elevator. Our true customers were actually the elevator mechanics whose lives we could make easier. It was to this group of people that SnapCab could be uniquely useful.

If the mechanic was happy, it meant everything. It meant that our intention to serve was coming alive in actual service. Our impact on another community was real. Our reason to exist as a company was confirmed.

This shift from passion-driven work to usefulness-driven work didn't diminish my love for what I did—it gave it greater meaning. When your work serves others, when it solves real problems and makes people's lives better, you discover a deeper satisfaction than personal fulfillment alone can provide.

This is the third principle of a Human Business: Focus on being useful. It's what happens when you combine what you love with what others genuinely need. But as we'll see in the next chapter, usefulness requires us to embrace something most businesses try to avoid: our problems and weaknesses.

Embrace Problems and Weaknesses

*Character cannot be developed in ease and quiet. Only through
experience of trial and suffering can the soul be strengthened,
vision cleared, ambition inspired, and success achieved.*
—HELEN KELLER

By 1998, we had problems—new problems. The team's workload was growing, and we were busier than ever before. All seven of us were focusing our efforts on fulfilling our contract with Otis.

Each cabinetmaker had his own set of skills, thoughts, and opinions on each project, and tensions began to rise as our daily workload became more intense. We were a bunch of individual cabinetmakers, after all—not a manufacturing team—and we had yet to establish the systems and processes that would guide us into efficient cooperation.

This caused a lot of issues, some annoying and others devastating. The work kept coming, but the problems were endless. I was always frustrated. My anger went home with me at the end of each workday, seven days a week.

Around this time, my friend Jonathan Simons, founder and owner of a company called Jonathan's Spoons, told me about a book: *The E-Myth Revisited* by Michael E. Gerber. Before reading the book, Jonathan believed that he was the only person who possessed the skills to make his product: handmade, one-of-a-kind wooden spoons. But after reading *The E-Myth Revisited*, he discovered that he could create systems and processes that would allow many craftspeople to come on board to make the spoons with equal attention to high quality.

I bought the book immediately. I had jobs to build, jobs to ship, and more work than hours to do it in. But I decided to go home and read. Having made a habit of rarely leaving work, I stayed home for three days, reading and studying, returning to the shop only when I had created a plan—hand-drawn on an easel.

Up to this point in life, I had only read the books I had been forced to read in school. But I was desperate for a change. Success had been coming our way, but we didn't really know how to deal with it. *The E-Myth Revisited* helped me realize that I had to work *on* the business instead of in it. I needed to create systems and processes that everyone could follow—or the company's success could not be sustained for long.

I stopped putting my attention on the daily operation of my company and devoted all of my time to building much-needed systems. I started with some simple ones and introduced them to my team. Quite quickly, we created a structure that had not been there before. The results were nothing short of stunning.

We had just hired a bunch of new people—landscapers with no cabinetmaking experience. As a consequence of the structure we had implemented, our fresh hires could enter the shop and see a group of defined work cells with instructions posted above each cell. What work was to be done and in what order to do it was obvious. The tools to do the work were right there in each work cell at the point of use. If a drill was missing, the shape of that drill had been drawn to indicate its home, a practice called **shadow boxing**. All of these small changes meant that employees with no prior experience could step in to do a high-quality job very quickly.

While it used to take a well-trained team eight hours to create one elevator interior, it now took a new team only six hours. The craftsman who had moved out of the shop into an engineering role looked out at the newbies in the shop with shock—how were newbies pulling this off? When the senior craftsmen combined their knowledge with the new systems, they found that they could reduce the completion time even more, so that one elevator interior now only took four hours to complete. The system, not the knowledge, became the source of our success. With the new standards in place, SnapCab moved out of the world of craft manufacturing and into the world of Lean manufacturing.

Despite the fact that the new systems made things easier to understand for all employees, not everyone was interested in using them—including an employee named Bob.

Bob had just finished an elevator interior job and shipped it off to Mexico, but he had failed to complete the final quality check before it was shipped. As a result, he hadn't noticed an error in the order: The pad buttons had been installed on the wrong panel. This defective product that had mistakenly left the facility and was delivered to the customer was what SnapCab refers to as an "escape."

This resulted in substantial waste. It took several days to correct. It meant additional working hours from both the delivery company that was shipping the parts and the elevator maintenance company installing the interior. The entire job had to be scrapped.

In Bob's defense, SnapCab's final quality check was not well-developed, thus not mistake-proof. At the time, I was frustrated, and I decided the best course of action was to yell at Bob. I figured that yelling would help Bob learn to use the system. That was my great solution. I yelled at Bob in front of everyone and proceeded to get into my car to go to the hardware store. A few minutes later, one of my employees called me to say Bob had quit and was heading out the door.

Even with the error, Bob was my best employee. I raced back to the office to apologize to him and beg him to stay. I even gave him a raise. I was confronted with the reality that yelling was simply not a viable solution. I needed a new way.

THE TWELVE STEPS AT WORK

Anger at work was not my only problem. Cheryl and I were still experiencing marriage challenges at home. By then, we had been married for seventeen years. I was forty. We had been to a number of marriage counselors but still hadn't managed to resolve our problems. One day, I saw a flyer for a presentation that was to be given by Peter Rhodes, a community member and acquaintance of mine. Peter, a retired parole officer turned counselor, was going to be speaking about the Twelve Steps of Alcoholics Anonymous. But instead of talking about the steps with regard to alcohol addiction, he would be using them as a tool for dealing with anger and resentment.

This was a novel idea. I had never heard of being addicted to anger and resentment, but I knew I regularly felt those emotions at home and at work. Curious to learn more, I decided to attend.

I had two awakenings—one during the talk and one afterward. First, I connected with the idea that I could apply a *system* to find relief from anger and resentment. Like the systems that restored the flow of work in my business, this system might release the flow of thought from the trappings of anger. My second awakening, which came sometime later, was more exciting than the first but also shocking. I learned that I was selfish.

This was the first time I had ever considered that my patterns of behavior and thinking stemmed from a selfish intention. Prior to hearing Peter speak, I denied this reality, choosing instead to blame other people. The Twelve Steps helped me see that my thinking had been self-serving in both my business and my marriage. My eyes were opened to the reality that I was not caring for the people around me. I finally had the words to understand it and the willingness to accept it.

I was so moved by Peter's presentation that I booked an individual counseling session with him. At the session, I asked Peter if he could help me with my marriage, but Peter said no. He told me that there was a chance Cheryl would leave me. Surprised by his frankness, I asked Peter what he *could* help me with. Peter offered to work with me individually as long as I was open to focusing on myself without concern for fixing my marriage, my wife, or other people. I had to be open to being honest about my ego and to doing the work of understanding and acting apart from my ego. I agreed.

Through our deeper work together, along with additional guidance and mentorship from a mutual friend, Dr. Ray Silverman, my perspective on my own thoughts, feelings, and actions started to change. I began observing and questioning my thinking while becoming more familiar with my ego. The results of this active reflection revealed that, when I relied on thinking from my ego, my actions were invariably "below the line." Jim Dethmer introduces this idea in his book, *The 15 Commitments of Conscious Leadership.*

Amazingly, below-the-line thinking seems to have a life of its own. It makes up all kinds of stories that I have been able to observe with my higher thinking. If I can take myself out of the situation, as if I am looking at my own story like I am reading a book or watching a movie, it is often made clear to me that I'm being driven by a selfish desire to look good, be admired, and get what I want. Peter helped me take a good look at my own mind.

Below-the-line thinking is the ego; above-the-line thinking is the higher self. This exercise, guided by a mentor I trusted, allowed me to identify the core problem—not just my superficial issues. Another way of saying it is that I investigated what was under the skin and found a selfish heart. But once I could see the truth, I was free to open up to having my thoughts raised.

Peter helped me realize that we are all selfish—it's part of being human. Better decisions can result from continually observing our own thoughts, feelings, and actions to see where they are truly coming from—even if we can't amend our behavior immediately.

EXERCISE: PAUSE AND REFLECT

Ready to practice a little self-reflection? Here is one simple question that we can ask ourselves: *What would be the caring thing to do?*

Doing this was difficult for me at first. It is still difficult, but it has become easier with practice. By acknowledging over and over again that my life is unmanageable and that I need help from what I call a higher power, my mind is open to change.

I try to convict my ego, like I'm in a courtroom, for any part I may have played in causing a problem. I do not aim to judge anyone else—only me. Once I am calm and sane, I apologize to the person whom I may have hurt, admitting my selfish actions. I have found that when I summon the courage to do this, the caring gesture brings out the best in me and the other person.

This practice reminds me of a *Seinfeld* episode where the character George Costanza does the opposite of what his instinct tells him to do, and the results are dramatically better than when he acts on impulse. Although dramatized, the episode sheds light on the poor outcomes that follow when we act impulsively on negativity over kindness.

When I'm angry at someone, I should do something kind for them instead of showing them how angry I am. Whenever I have done this, it has always gone much better than when I have let my negative feelings be known. This doesn't mean I have to suppress my negative emotions; but I can be mindful of when, how, and with whom I express them. I can be mindful of my body. When my face is hot and my chest is tight, that's my cue to keep my mouth shut and go for a walk. My ego wants to teach someone a lesson—right now—but if I wait until I am calm, I gain access to the influence of my higher self. I can deal with the issue at hand in a constructive way.

Along with Peter's guidance, the guidance of another mentor has helped me learn to interact without anger leading the charge. Ray Silverman taught me that whenever I want to share my thoughts or feelings with another person, I can ask myself three questions: *Is what I'm about to say kind? Is it true? Is it useful?* These simple questions guide me to clear answers and give me a better chance at speaking my thoughts from a considerate heart.

Recognizing the physical signs of anger, such as a tight chest and hot face, is crucial in managing your emotions. People's bodies respond to strong emotions in different ways. Just as astronauts train in hypobaric chambers to be able to recognize their individual responses when their oxygen is dropping, we can train ourselves to know when emotions are taking over. As Peter Rhodes points out, using a raised voice and anger may force compliance, but it doesn't foster genuine alignment or relationships. Instead, when you notice these cues, it's wise to pause and step away. Returning to the situation calmly allows you to communicate logically and respectfully, building trust and cooperation through reasoned explanation rather than forceful emotion.

THE START OF A HUMAN BUSINESS

I remember one time that Cheryl and I went to marriage counseling. Cheryl brought up an issue that we were having, and I admitted to her and to the counselor that I had been acting selfishly around that issue. They were very surprised by my answer, but it was the truth. I started to let my wife be herself, without interfering with who she was. She didn't need to orchestrate her life around me. Communicating this realization to my wife was transformative. As I expressed my ego concerns less, leaving Cheryl in freedom to be Cheryl without my judgment, the tension between us began to ease.

Before meeting with Peter, I had been in denial. I was asleep. First, I needed to wake up to see the problem. Before I could fix the problem, I had to admit the problem: The problem was me. Until then, I had never felt myself to be anything other than in the right. I knew the way to go, and it was my job to teach you my way. But when my denial lifted, I could see that I had been preoccupied with what was right at the expense of others' well-being. I had been controlling other people with anger to get what I wanted. I didn't want to do that anymore; it didn't work. I succeeded only in pushing other people away. For the first time in my life, **I considered my intention and how it would affect people.** In other words, **I committed to kindness first.**

This decision was really the start of a Human Business.

A few months later, Bob made another mistake. This time, he shipped a ceiling to Hawaii without pulling back the plastic protective film for a final quality check. If he had, he would have realized that the ceiling had a mirrored finish instead of the intended brushed finish. The customer was unhappy.

Despite this expensive and time-consuming error, my response to Bob was different from what it had been before. By this time, I had come to understand that people are led by what they love. Punishing people for making honest mistakes only creates fear. It doesn't incentivize them to be productive. In fact, it has the opposite effect and *actively harms* productivity.

I knew that Bob was a good worker, and that he hadn't made the mistake through maliciousness or through a lack of caring. So, instead of yelling, I thanked Bob and invited him to be part of the solution. Bob loves doing a good job and being appreciated—and he also loves his wife! I chose to lead by finding a solution where those loves could be combined.

We needed someone to go down to Hawaii to fix the ceiling anyway, so why not send Bob, along with his wife? It took Bob one day to fix the mistake and six days to enjoy a vacation. The way I handled this situation gave Bob the energy to continue growing and doing great work at SnapCab.

This marked the beginning of rewarding people for their mistakes, a practice SnapCab does to this day. Of course, we don't send everyone to Hawaii when they make a mistake, but since then, employees have been encouraged to report mistakes so the team can work together to come up with a mistake-proof solution.

Before he even left for Hawaii, Bob came up with a checklist system that would help prevent anyone from making the same mistake he had made. He was thrilled about the opportunity to not only go on vacation, but to be a part of a solution that benefited the whole business.

Here's the takeaway: Before I knew I was selfish, I ran a conventional business. After I knew I was selfish, I started building something altogether different, something human.

THE BREAKTHROUGH AT ITO

Not long after signing the big contract with Otis, Otis sent me to Connecticut to participate in the Achieving Competitive Excellence program that was being held at Ito University—by United Technologies Corporation. Over the span of a full week, I learned about Lean manufacturing, a production practice developed and popularized by Toyota that is associated with continuous process improvement and waste reduction.

At Ito, I learned something important: Because highlighting mistakes is conducive to intentionally fixing the systems that caused them, **the gold is in the problems**. No problems, no **gold**. Noting that my instructors referred to mistakes and problems as "turnbacks," I later adopted the same terminology at SnapCab. A **turnback** is simply anything that hinders the flow of work.

What's essential to this approach, though, is that the people involved have to be open and communicative when turnbacks occur. If someone makes a mistake, that person must not hide it from the team. This requires all team members to commit to receiving the turnback report with care so that each employee can benefit from an environment where people can be vulnerable with one another.

This idea resonated with me deeply, given my personal awakening to my own weaknesses. At Ito, I was realizing how essential it was to be open about my weaknesses with my colleagues and customers. Two seemingly separate worlds—the personal and the professional—were coming together.

This was not bad news. On the contrary, it was good. I was coming to see that if the gold is in the mistakes, then our mistakes are essential for growth. They are opportunities to be better, personally and professionally. Personal failure can be uncomfortable, but once we accept that problems will always occur, it's not so difficult to fail. If we look through the lens of continuous improvement, we open ourselves, and possibly our whole business, to fresh insight or a more efficient process. We may even be surprised to find a deepening mutual trust with our coworkers. Dealing with problems openly is essential to community building at SnapCab.

THE GOLD IS IN THE WASTE

After returning from Ito, I incorporated a number of Lean manufacturing practices into SnapCab's systems. We improved on some of the methods we were already practicing—shadow boxing—and introduced new methods. One such method involved taping pathways to the floor, which improved our collective understanding of how the work flows through the factory. We adopted these simple improvements to help everyone remove waste and work toward mistake-proof systems.

Years later, I traveled to Japan with a team from SnapCab to learn about Lean manufacturing directly from Ritsuo Shingo, who was the former president of Toyota China and the son of Dr. Shigeo Shingo, an early advocate and leader in the development of the Toyota Production System. I've been on four trips to Japan, all with Paul Akers, the last two being led by him. I've found Paul to be the best teacher of Japanese culture and Lean manufacturing. He is a leader in the Lean manufacturing world and author of *2 Second Lean* and many other books on the topic. We ended up building on our introduction to Ritsuo, later enjoying an opportunity to host him at SnapCab at our US headquarters on a tour that Paul organized. The result of his visit was another round of new improvements to our systems and processes, though we were later surprised to learn that SnapCab had impressed our guest before changes were even made.

Paul asked Ritsuo after his visit to North America what his favorite company had been. Ritsuo said, "SnapCab." He experienced aspects of the Human Business described in this book. One simple system that Ritsuo had liked a lot was called the Gemba board, a method for capturing turnbacks (issues) that relies on a set of physical boards hanging on the walls of each department. Named for a Japanese term that translates to "the actual place," these Gemba boards display turnbacks for all to see and provide a daily meeting place for each team to review issues and share information about what is interrupting the flow of work.

Getting even more specific, the Gemba board displays sticky notes on which team members have logged recent turnbacks. Not every turnback is acted upon; rather, the Gemba board is a place to uncover issues and monitor trends. If there is a way to fix the turnback, the manager will wait until after the meeting to work with a team of employees to plan solutions to the problem. At SnapCab, we call these solutions "**countermeasures**" to leave room for future improvements to the same turnback.

What Ritsuo liked the most about our Gemba boards was how we reduced fear by rewarding employees for identifying mistakes and involving them in creating mistake-proof solutions.

At SnapCab, each time an employee reports a turnback, they receive a carnival ticket from their manager. The employees report turnbacks and collect tickets throughout the month. Then, at the monthly **all-company meeting**, the tickets are counted company-wide, and the team member who has the most tickets that month wins a prize.

The ticket component is not a traditional Gemba practice; it's an idea I learned about a few years later that makes reporting turnbacks more enjoyable. Each ticket says "Admit One," an acknowledgment of admitting our own mistake.

When it's time to address a specific turnback, the employee who reported the original turnback is consulted for possible countermeasures. If the employee is left out of this part of the process and is simply told what to do, the employee is disempowered; they may not be invested in making the improvement a success. But when they are empowered to come up with an initial countermeasure, they have ownership around the process and investment in the improvement's success. If the first countermeasure isn't effective, the problem will reoccur and will continue to show up on the Gemba board until the core issue has been fixed. In this way, our system is a self-healing one, just like the human body.

With the Gemba boards, everyone gets a voice, and no single person is responsible for a problem. In fact, we aim to blame the system, not the person. In the case that there is actually a system in place, but it wasn't used because of a lack of training, we can report that too.

Addressing the issue without blaming each other is supported by SnapCab's first core value: Be kind. Admitting any part we have played in contributing to the problem is supported by the second value: Be authentic. An environment with open communication, free from shaming, leads to healthy collaboration, which helps us all to be useful, our third value.

In many cases, a turnback exists because of a deeper **root cause**; the turnback becomes a beacon for a lack of work instructions, employee training, or standardization of a process. Without the beacon, we are blind. We need the beacon to know where to mine for gold.

HONESTY ATTRACTS HELP

Over time, my three mentors from ABG Consulting noticed how much SnapCab was growing and encouraged me to join a business group to learn about leadership from other CEOs. I had no formal business background, but I was willing to follow their advice because I felt ill-equipped to run the business that SnapCab was evolving into.

We had just moved SnapCab from our first, smaller building of around eleven thousand square feet to a much larger, forty-thousand-square-foot location. We thought we had enough money to make the move and grow, but it soon became obvious that we were sinking. I didn't know how to respond.

Dick Brickman suggested that I join Vistage, an executive peer advisory group. This group of local business leaders met monthly to discuss each other's experiences and offer advice. Right from the beginning, I was clear with the group members. I told them I had a lot to learn about running a business. I was honest about my weaknesses, specifically around accounting, and sought advice to solve my problem with cash flow. I was authentic with them about the state of my business. It would have been more comfortable to sit back and pretend to have all the answers. Instead, I admitted to the group what I didn't understand.

This choice was pivotal in getting the help I needed, despite my ego creeping in with concern that I would look incompetent. Susan Smith, the chair of my Vistage group, told me that it was a real strength to recognize and share weaknesses. At first, I thought she was joking or patronizing me, but over time, I realized she was right.

Once the group understood my challenges, four members offered to visit SnapCab to see if they could help. The group reviewed the current cash flow system, interviewed employees, and determined that SnapCab's cash flow would improve dramatically if the company requested deposits from customers.

Requesting deposits saved our business. It wasn't an industry norm to ask for deposits, and I felt a lot of pressure from my sales team to reconsider the idea. They feared we would lose customers if we made the change. But I needed to do something, so I accepted the suggestion. I didn't have the wisdom on my own to know how to fix my problem, but fortunately, I did have the wisdom to know to ask for help. Asking for help and accepting it—that was my part to play.

In spite of many positive experiences with Vistage, I couldn't shake the feeling that I was out of my league. The other CEOs I met with each month had strong educational backgrounds, or at least strong business experience. By contrast, I struggled with learning disabilities, had a background in woodworking, and hadn't completed my community college degree. Even though I was learning useful information at each meeting, my confidence was low; I started to wonder whether I should be leading SnapCab at all.

I thought back to the way I felt when I first started in business. At the time, I felt invincible. I later realized I felt that way because I didn't know what I didn't know. As the years passed and my business progressed, the gaps in my knowledge became more apparent, and I allowed them to make me feel inadequate.

This ongoing low confidence led to many years of me inviting both internal and external people to come in and lead. Over about a decade, I welcomed in four different leaders who I felt had the education or business experience to take SnapCab to the next level.

However, each time I took a step back from the role of company leader and instead acted as the supportive business owner, SnapCab would begin to veer off track. The original vision was replaced, over and over again, with another vision that subordinated common institutional knowledge to expert head knowledge, simplicity to complexity, or usefulness to profit. The business would always begin to lose its essential features.

So, I started to question whether bringing in another leader was really the missing piece that SnapCab needed. Those other leaders had the credentials, but their plans to direct the company were not compatible with my vision. I wondered if perhaps my vision had a higher value than I was giving it credit for.

What I can give myself credit for is being authentic about my weakness: I did need leadership and organizational help. But, after twenty years of experimentation, I can see that I was not being authentic about my strength. I had denied the vision I had been given in my role as CEO. I denied my call to steward the business into relying on common institutional knowledge over expert head knowledge, simplicity above complexity, and usefulness above profit. I abdicated my stewardship role to other leaders who rejected the defining features of SnapCab in favor of their own visions for the company. The fact that this happened over and over again was a result of my low confidence—my weakness as a leader—a fact made easier to digest by the rich learning that has emerged from the mire.

INTEGRATING FLAWS

I have learned about life and leadership not by achievement but by repeated experience with weakness, problems, and failure. Tolerating failure and continuing on anyway is like building a muscle. We don't build our muscles by not using them. We don't learn to be good sailors by sailing calm waters. We build our muscles by using them; we learn to be good sailors by sailing rough seas. We grow as leaders if we choose to face the next challenge head-on and accept the outcome, whatever it may be.

Think about someone in your life whom you admire. Do you feel closest to them when you are in awe of an amazing talent they have? Or do you connect with them when you find out that they, too, are flawed? Perhaps you feel both are important, but I've learned that I don't connect with others through strengths alone. I feel a strong connection when someone is willing to let their flaws be seen. This motivates me to practice openness in spite of the risk it requires. And my gratitude runs deep when someone sees my shortcomings and treats me with grace and respect all the same.

My attention to flaws goes beyond my rela-

tionships with people. It has informed my approach to product design since the early days of making elevator interiors. To this day, our installation process accounts for the fact that all elevator cabs are flawed in one way or another. Installation of our panels isn't thwarted by slanted ceilings or uneven walls; the product is designed to "expect" the flaws and accommodate them. What might at first present itself as a problem is actually just a reality that we accept as a given: Slanted ceilings are fine. Uneven walls are fine. It's no one's fault—it just is. Our system can handle it just fine.

My daughter Carla, who has witnessed the growth of SnapCab over the course of her life, made a comment that reminded me of what I am doing with this business model. A member of the SnapCab team herself—director of pod architecture and design—she said, "Don't you see? You have considered that all people, products, and processes are flawed. It's all flawed! You've designed a business with the under-standing that all of these things are flawed, and accommodating those flaws is a key part of growing the company."

Oh yeah, I realized. The flaws are part of the plan. A Human Business takes into account that everything is flawed—the employees, the suppliers, the customers, and the products. We have systems, processes, and principles that are prepared to include them as part of the business strategy. That's where the gold lies.

WHEN THE STUDENT IS READY, THE WASTE APPEARS

I'd like to return now to how continuous improvement in the workplace depends on the continuous improvement of our minds. What I found in my work with Peter Rhodes is that the removal of waste from our minds can lead to the removal of waste at work. Let me be more specific.

If I lash out in anger at a coworker, the bigger turnback is in my reaction, not in the surface issue. I call my own toxic reaction "waste" in need of removal. If I am invested in self-awareness, this situation is an opportunity to take my destructive energy and use it to grow as a person. It is a chance to make the choice to build a constructive relationship with my coworker. I can do this by taking responsibility for my outburst and initiating a repair—all before addressing the more visible work issue.

Let's compare the problem to another form of waste: manure. This is a comparison I learned from Ray Silverman.

Manure is necessary, but it can be harmful if used incorrectly. If I keep manure in my house, I'll likely get sick. But if I use it outside as fertilizer for my soil, I can grow a beautiful garden. Just as we have a choice in how to use manure, we have a choice in how to use the waste that comes from problems. The results for each scenario are the same: disease or growth.

OUT OF HIDING, INTO AWARENESS

Before a child understands object permanence, they will hold a blanket or cushion over their face and believe they have disappeared; but their torso, legs, and feet are in plain sight. The child thinks they're invisible, but everyone else knows the hiding is temporary.

I relate this experience back to people who attempt to hide their problems and weaknesses. The harder they work at hiding their faults, the more obvious they are to everyone around them. For example, when an employee causes a lot of trouble for their teammates, and management doesn't want to address it, there's a partial mask over the situation. But it is still a very clear, obvious problem for those experiencing it.

Let's bring it back from the organizational level to the personal level. Let's bring it back to our minds. What it comes down to is above-the-line and below-the-line thinking. If we're engaged with the ego, we're acting below the line. If we're being open about our faults, we're willing to work on them, and we're considering other people, we are acting above the line.

We can also be above the line by simply acknowledging that we're acting below the line. In this way, we are elevating our consciousness and expanding our self-awareness, one humbling experience at a time.

When I understood the power of observing my own thinking and accepting that not all my own thinking is correct and true, I noticed how often I had been blaming others for not fulfilling my requests. In other words, I came into the harsh light of reality. It was Peter, in one of our counseling sessions, who introduced me to an idea that really woke me up. "All expectations," he said, "are premeditated resentments." When I started to really scrutinize where I could be at fault, and then shift my responses accordingly, my relationships transformed. I can see most clearly, I think, when I consciously notice my ego engaging. I might be feeling defensive, for instance, if someone has a better idea than me. But when I am able to detach from my ego, I am able to make the best decision for the company, or the relationship, or both.

Just because we are willing to see the truth about our ego mind doesn't mean it's easy to change our behavior in our relationships. But there are resources to help us adopt a practice of responding differently. The book *Crucial Conversations* has been influential in the way I express my concerns. When initiating a sensitive conversation, it helps to communicate to my colleague that I have a story in my head that

I want to share. Like this: "I have this story in my head, and I'd like to talk to you about it to see if you also think it's true." Sharing the concern this way helps us to detach from it while we work together to figure out the truth. It's one way to remove blame from the issue, while encouraging collaborative discussion and problem-solving.

What I can do next is take a step back and take some time to allow the feeling to run its course. I often go for a walk or a drive to reflect on the gratitude I have to be in a position where I get to work on this issue with my coworker. Space away from the situation gives me time to decide whether acting on my initial thoughts would be a relationship builder. Taking the time to reflect gives me space to reframe the value of our relationship overall. Then, when I return, I have more appreciation for the person. Instead of focusing only on what's going wrong, I have a fuller picture of the truth. I have perspective, and with perspective, I feel calm. This approach is less reactive and more productive, but, like most things, it's a practice.

EXERCISE: HOW TO FIND SELF-AWARENESS

In a state of calm, call to mind an issue—a problem at work. It's a problem you're not responsible for. Maybe it's not a big deal, just a tense conversation in the kitchen by the coffee maker. Or maybe it's something more visible, a public scene that has taken permanence in your mental landscape. When you see it in your mind's eye, you feel defensive. You want it known that you are not to blame.

Now ask yourself one simple question: *Is there anything I could have done differently?* By taking time to reflect, you are yielding to the possibility that there is something within your control that you may be able to amend. You are practicing what the Japanese call **hansei**—a neutral way to reflect on yourself and your actions. This term is almost synonymous with "spiritual work."

BE OPEN; BE AUTHENTIC

It really makes an impression on me when someone is open about a specific weakness.

One employee confessed in his first interview at SnapCab that he had trouble managing his calendar, affecting his ability to meet deadlines. *Wow*, I thought. *That's refreshing. A real weakness admitted.* He had offered us the gift of the truth, which allowed our leadership team to become aware of a possible issue ahead of its arrival. A willingness to be vulnerable allowed us to plan for support in that specific area. And we did, in fact, hire him. He works for SnapCab to this day.

We have covered a lot of ground in this chapter. It began with the problems that opened me up to receive help, both at work and at home. **It was only with the willingness to pause and reflect that I could make the changes that led to improvement.** The new systems on the factory floor could not have been instated without my choice to stop, observe, and acknowledge the turnbacks. Likewise, a renewed connection with my wife could not have been established without my choice to stop, observe, and acknowledge the unproductive thoughts in my head.

This choice to pause, reflect, and admit what's going wrong is still not easy more than twenty-five years later—it's hard on the ego. But when we practice honesty about our weaknesses, we are practicing authenticity. When we're authentic, other people can show up to fill the gaps. When we're authentic, we give others the chance to showcase their strengths and solve problems when our own strength is failing. What results is personal humility, increased trust, and a more interdependent community of people.

This new vision for work, in which we are vulnerable with each other, only works when this practice is shared across the community. If one person is regularly open about their weaknesses and another condemns them for it, the condemnation can result in imbalance, separation, and a toxic environment. In other words, the end of kindness. The end of caring.

Maintaining our emphasis on caring means relying on a strong system to attract the right people to our community in the first place. Candidates must fit this caring profile. And if there are people whose behavior threatens the well-being of others, we can activate a performance improvement plan (PIP, explained later) to educate and encourage them to embrace our company values—or to give them the opportunity to find employment in another place that suits them. This frees them to find belonging elsewhere and frees SnapCab to fill the position with a different person. In other words, it's a win-win. Ultimately, each of us at SnapCab must continue to be open with each other, sharing our problems and weaknesses so that our community continues to be made up of people who have this value in common.

Model Your Business After the Human Form: Part I

Organizations are living systems, not machines. They have the capacity to learn, adapt, and grow—just like the human body.
—PETER SENGE

By 2008, SnapCab had become a much more developed version of its original conception, and so had I. Inspired by lessons I had learned from reading *The E-Myth Revisited*, Cheryl and I began dreaming of expanding to Canada. We wanted to build a home on Wolfe Island, Ontario, and start a second SnapCab location in Kingston, a twenty-minute ferry ride away. I had always maintained strong ties to the area, having spent many summers at my mother's cottage on the island; and Cheryl could be just a few hours away from her hometown.

I had a strong leadership team, and I felt that the Warrington location and its eighty-plus employees would be in great hands if I were to take some time to focus on a new business in Kingston.

We had spent years building an operating system that housed the systems and processes at our Warrington location. We dubbed the operating system the DNA File System, or the DNA. This operating system is a simple electronic file folder system and file index, created in Excel. The idea is that everyone can access the files and resources they need to do their work. It provides a catch-all for the many documents the company has and continues to create. It serves as an institutional memory bank, with a clear notation for who is in charge of the document. It is searchable by keyword. It helps prevent reinventing the wheel.

I wanted it to be comprehensive, and something that could be transplanted to start another branch. Rather than wasting time searching the entire database for what they need, managers can use the DNA system to quickly access certain parts of the DNA that pertain directly to their team. It also provides a concise summary of what they are accountable and responsible for.

Along with departmental documents and SOPs for company systems, the DNA also holds the company's strategic plan, job descriptions, roles and responsibilities, career paths, educational resources, and more. Most importantly, it preserves our core values—be kind, be authentic, and be useful.

THE BIRTH OF A SECOND COMPANY

In 2009, we made the move to Canada. I initially worked from our rented apartment in Kingston, making monthly seven-hour drives to Warrington to stay connected to the US team.

More opportunities, more change, and more growth followed the establishment of our second SnapCab location. Soon after moving to Canada, I established the Kingston Executive Group (KEG), a business leadership group similar to the Vistage executive peer advisory group I had participated in back in Pennsylvania. I had learned so much participating in that business group that I thought it could be a useful resource for other local business owners in Kingston. Plus, I didn't know many local people, so I figured that starting this group would help me meet other like-minded entrepreneurs in the area.

It was at KEG that I met some of my future employees and friends. I met Hugh Roberts, a building developer, who would later come on board with SnapCab to help develop new products.

After running things alone in Canada for a couple of years, I invited Jon Kerr to join me. He had worked throughout our Warrington factory and was highly committed to SnapCab and to customer service. Jon had always gone above and beyond the call of duty, including one time, specifically, when he drove hours out of his way to fix a mixed-up order. I trusted Jon. I respected his earnest approach to work.

I approached Jon with the idea of moving up to Canada to help me start the new business. After quick consideration, Jon accepted the opportunity to join me in giving the Canadian venture a try.

By 2013, Jon was living in Kingston and helping me build the business. After months of searching for a manufacturing facility in the Kingston area, we found one. Jon and I secured the location and began to set up shop.

The market was very unwelcoming at first. But, despite the setbacks, Jon persevered. He did a phenomenal job overseeing the development of the new location. After a short time, I offered him a raise. Remarkably, Jon turned it down. I couldn't believe it. Jon said he didn't want a raise until the Canadian company made a profit. To me, that is someone who really has his heart in it. He put the company's success before his own financial success. He put the SnapCab community first.

Jon acted as a true member of a team. He allowed me to lead and followed directions when asked. He managed projects but ensured they were in alignment with the overall vision for the company. Even when there were turnbacks, they could be recognized and addressed because he and I collaborated as one unit.

In 2015, we worked together to purchase a much larger manufacturing facility across the road, where SnapCab Canada still operates to this day. Along with the fifty-six-thousand-square-foot facility in Warrington, Pennsylvania, this new thirty-six-thousand-square-foot facility in Canada allowed us to expand our useful operation, creating space for growth that improved our capacity for servicing our customers.

This experience with Jon exemplified one of the core principles I was learning about organizational health: **When people are aligned with a shared intention and work together as parts of a whole body, extraordinary things become possible.** Jon wasn't just an employee—he was a vital part of SnapCab Canada, functioning in perfect harmony with the vision. But as I would soon discover, maintaining that alignment across a growing organization would prove to be one of my greatest challenges.

NEW LEADERSHIP IN A GROWING COMPANY

Fortunately, not long afterward, I met Sahiza Hossenbaccus, and we brought her on as SnapCab Canada's chief financial officer (CFO). In a very short time, she grew into not only the CFO of both locations but also the general manager at the Canadian location. Also, in 2023, she stepped into the role of president for both the Canadian and US locations.

Although Sahiza was an instrumental addition to the team in 2018, I needed more leaders. We interviewed Kyle Mullin, originally an engineer with General Electric and later an operations manager for an Amazon warehouse. He certainly had the experience that I was looking for in a leader, so I contacted him for an interview. After getting to know the type of human being he was, I offered him a position.

I think Kyle recognized that SnapCab did things in a different way. We had a human-centered approach that was different from what he had experienced at larger corporations. Sometime after the hiring process, Kyle reflected on his experience in the job interview with me:

"Anytime I've approached a job interview, I've always focused on speaking to my specific experiences and accomplishments. The interview is the one time where you have to brag about yourself and talk yourself up. My SnapCab interview was so unique. Speaking with Glenn, I remember thinking, *Don't you care about my accomplishments? You seem to care more about me as a person and finding out about who I am—what motivates me to get out of bed in the morning. You want to know more about my personality. Do you [only] care how I'm going to fit in with*

> *the people here, or do you care about what I'm going to bring to the table?*
>
> I realized, over time, that it was about how I fit in. While it didn't really make sense to me at first, it makes absolute sense to me now. SnapCab was totally ahead of the curve in looking at personalities and how someone might mesh with the culture of the company as opposed to how much efficiency they were able to gain at their last job. It was extremely enlightening."

THE BIRTH OF A NEW PRODUCT LINE

In 2016, SnapCab exhibited at the AIA (American Institute of Architects) Conference on Architecture, as it had for many years, but this time it displayed its elevator interior products as well as the new SnapCab Portal, both featuring Corning Gorilla Glass. Our exhibit received a lot of attention and excitement from trade show attendees. One attendee in particular was looking for something a little bit different.

A consultant for what was at that time one of the world's largest coworking companies, WeWork, said to us that he was seeking office pods for coworking spaces. The structure of our elevator interior products was similar to that of an office pod. All our existing design needed to become a pod was exterior walls, a door, and a few other components. The consultant asked if we would be interested in developing a new office pod product that could be used for the coworking company. He needed 1,650 units per year. I thought it could be worthwhile to give it a shot—to try something new, see if a new product could be useful, and see if we could meet this new market need. After all, SnapCab's aforementioned DNA system meant our manufacturing system was scalable.

I decided to act right away. That weekend, rather than waiting for our busy engineers to have time to draw a prototype, I bought some tracing paper, a T square, triangles, and some pencils and erasers. I spent Saturday and Sunday working with Hugh Roberts, SnapCab's research and development manager, on designing an office pod prototype. Again, this new product design featured SnapCab's ILP system, which allowed us the flexibility to quickly design an innovative product. On Monday, we started building the pod prototype based on the drawing. We finished within the week.

That Sunday, the consultant from the AIA show flew across the country to visit us, and we presented to him a complete prototype based on the proposal he had made just one week before. The consultant loved it.

As it turned out, the coworking company that had considered purchasing SnapCab pods decided to look for a product with a lower price tag, much less than it would cost to make a high-quality SnapCab pod. By this time, the team and I could see that there was a demand for the product, and that was all we needed to know to press on with a plan of our own.

The SnapCab pods featured replaceable panels, heavy-duty casters for easy mobility, aluminum extrusions that allowed us to connect pods to each other, and other features that were unique to this new market. Despite having lost the coworking customer, we were optimistic. We knew there was a growing market for flexible, high-quality pods.

That summer, SnapCab exhibited the new pod product at AIA and received a great deal of attention from attendees and large companies alike. Panasonic, for instance, approached us to share that they had upcoming projects for which they could use our collaboration.

SnapCab also exhibited at NeoCon, North America's largest commercial interior design show, and our new SnapCab pod won a Best of NeoCon award.

Our new product was taking off. It was amazing to see the interest, even in this first design, upon which we have since improved. Our team was energized by what the future had in store for SnapCab.

We didn't abandon our core identity—we were still using the same ILP system, the same manufacturing DNA, and the same values. SnapCab was evolving to meet a market need we hadn't anticipated. The question was whether all parts of our organization would remain aligned during this growth.

SNAPCAB FALLS APART

As it turned out, things were not as they seemed. When my family and I first moved to Canada, I had confidence in starting the second SnapCab location because I believed the company had adopted and maintained the set of proven, scalable systems from which our future growth would stem.

In 2017, though, when interest in SnapCab pods was growing, I started to see that the foundation of the company—the documented systems and processes I *thought* were intact in our US facility—had eroded. For nearly a decade, my attention had been focused on growing our second business in Canada. During this time, some of the systems and processes had been deliberately abandoned, while others had faded away gradually.

I was asleep to the daily operations of the US factory because I was so focused on getting the Canadian facility up and running. We had been making money in the US, so I thought we were doing fine. In fact, we had been growing so quickly that we made the Inc. 5000 list in eight different years. But I started to pay more attention when I learned that we were having turnback after turnback.

It was painful to acknowledge that our systems had atrophied over time. The company was being led in multiple directions by **head knowledge**—invisible knowledge that was subject to change and was dependent on human memory. **There was no more order in the company—it was no longer led by a foundation of documented systems and processes**, as it had been originally. **The company was no longer acting as an interconnected organism—a healthy human body. Instead, the shared instructions for useful activity and growth were gone, and in their place was malignant growth—tumors and disease.**

This realization was devastating. I had spent years building SnapCab on a foundation of documented systems and shared values—a clear DNA that every employee could access and follow. But what happens when that foundation crumbles? What happens when departments stop communicating with each other, when they forget the core principles and processes that should guide their actions? I was about to learn that lesson the hard way.

SnapCab's original business model for elevator interiors was simple. It included just four models, featuring horizontal panels that fit all elevators universally and were simple for elevator mechanics to install. They had been designed to be the right product for 80 percent of the market's elevator interior needs. However, during the time I was away, the US leadership team, in cooperation with the sales team, had yielded to the requests of architects, neglecting the needs of those that we had promised to serve: elevator maintenance companies. SnapCab had veered away from the original business model with the explicit intention of making higher sales.

I had been aware that this was the direction in which the team wanted to move, but I was slow to jump on board. The new direction wasn't in alignment with SnapCab's original business model, and I wasn't clear on how it could scale. However, the team showed me the financials, and the company was making more money than ever before. Surely this way of doing business was working.

It was hard to argue against the people who were in charge of running the business because I needed and trusted them. We were making money, which, I decided, must be proof that I was off base in my hesitation to accept the new plan. So I decided to go along with changing the model to align with the team's updated vision, allowing an influx of complex designs not in alignment with our original goal that had, in the old days, defined the value of our product for the installers and end users. The original model was simple to order, manufacture, and install.

Architects wanted vertical panels and lots of materials. They wanted to be the designers of the elevator interiors, making each job unique with its own unproven designs and accompanying challenges, including longer installation time. Our four standard models swelled to over forty, many of which did not fit the simple-to-install standard. Even then, architects would come up with their own ideas, leaving us with an overwhelming number of custom jobs. We've now established a custom department to handle these projects. And I'm working on a book on the business of elevator interiors that gives architects and designers all the information they need to specify products that are viable to manufacture and that meet code.

But SnapCab didn't have repeatable systems and processes in place to outline how to build all of these new models. We didn't have installation instructions for the vast number of custom jobs either because they were each unique. Worst of all, many models were no longer installed in a single day, our signature service. Sometimes, it would take two or three days to install—a less snappy SnapCab experience than elevator mechanics had enjoyed in the beginning.

Ultimately, we were breaking our original promise to elevator maintenance companies—to provide elevator interior products that could be installed within a day. In other words, we were no longer being authentic. We were trying to serve two customers at the same time: our original customer—the elevator maintenance mechanics—and the architectural market, which desired complicated jobs. This made it difficult to keep our promise of providing simple-to-install solutions. We had diverted our attention from service to sales. We became a company that had abandoned the identity we had claimed as an antidote to the profit-focused motives of conventional business.

Twenty years after innovating the ILP system as an answer to an industry problem, we found ourselves *inside* of the industry problem. To top it off, we had lost touch with the values that had nourished our workplace culture: Be kind, be authentic, and be useful. These were nice on paper, but they no longer animated the spirit of the company. This raises the point that whatever business model you have, you should consider whether you are on track with your mission and your value proposition. Any business can go off track. Don't lose sight of your core competency. You might expand the scope of what your product or service does beyond your competency, only to grab more revenue but fail at creating real value.

MAJOR TURNBACKS CREATE
PAIN AND CONFLICT

These issues originally came to my attention when I learned that full elevator jobs had to be scrapped and rebuilt three times over because SnapCab had no process to manufacture the design effectively. I started to see the disconnect between the products that were being sold and our ability to manufacture those products. The only reason I hadn't been aware of the waste at first was that the company had been charging the customer enough to cover the costs.

There was no way around it. It was terrible. I drove from Kingston to Warrington and held a large meeting with a representative from each department. Together, we outlined the entire process, starting at the beginning (being awarded a job) and going all the way to the end (shipping a job). What we noticed was that many things were out of alignment between departments.

We recognized a major disconnect between the sales team and the engineering and manufacturing teams. The sales team liked selling complex, expensive elevator interiors, but engineering and manufacturing had incredible difficulty making them. The engineering and manufacturing teams preferred the standardized models, but the sales team wasn't attracted to selling them.

Standard models, the sales team explained, required the company to make many more sales to yield the same revenue that just one sale of a custom model would bring in.

Custom models, the manufacturing team explained, slowed the system down, since the factory processes that the company had established did not support custom orders with attributes outside of the standard options. Continuing with custom jobs hurt the manufacturing department and caused us to break our promise to our customers.

The tension between teams was palpable.

Related issues continued to surface as we took time to spotlight each phase of a given order. It became clear, for example, that SnapCab hadn't updated its pricing for years; the system was now too complicated. The only person who knew how to update the quoting software had left the company, leaving the pricing problem unsolved. On top of that, the company's DNA system, which held the comprehensive store of systems and processes that would enable SnapCab to scale, was no longer in use by the majority of employees. It was a shock for me to see so clearly that the company was largely running on head knowledge, on invisible memory subject to error and to the whims of individual employees. We were like a body with multiple heads working at cross-purposes. A kind of mutated business monster. Our shared foundation of institutional knowledge, originally informing the entire organizational body with sound instructions, had eroded.

I was not the only one in distress. Everyone in that meeting could see the overwhelming misalignment between departments and the impact of a widespread breakdown of systems. It was clear that this current way of doing business—a mutation of the original model—was not scalable and that the company was doomed to illness or worse if its systems did not receive the caring attention they needed. For health to be restored across departments, we had to return to our original business model, which had subordinated profit to usefulness. And we had to repair our DNA to restore common access to the institutional knowledge that could nurture our community into the future.

This experience taught me something crucial about organizational health: **It's not enough to simply organize people into departments and give them titles. For a company to function, every employee must have access to the same foundational knowledge—the same core instructions, values, and purpose. When that foundation**

breaks down or gets forgotten, the company becomes sick. The departments stop working together, and what was once a unified organization becomes a collection of competing parts, each pursuing its own agenda without regard for the health of the whole.

TAKING OWNERSHIP OF MY MISTAKES

I admit that when I moved to Canada, I abdicated leadership of the US facility to the general manager at the time and his supporting leadership staff. I wasn't paying close attention to what was going on outside of my immediate awareness. I wasn't nurturing and communicating my vision for the US company because I had been content enough in hearing reports that the company was making money, that it was doing well. But I had been asleep to the full picture. I had not realized that, in fact, our tried-and-true SOPs had fallen out of use.

What I can see, upon reflection, is that I mistook making money for having a well-run company. It's true that money can be an indicator of success, but by itself, it can distract from the true health of the company. SnapCab was bringing money in, but we crashed. A company without a shared vision and shared systems begins to unravel. And that is what happened at SnapCab.

There was more to our unraveling. For close to a decade, I had been worried about putting myself in a leadership position because I was concerned about falling into an egotistical entrepreneur trap. I had not wanted to become a leader who believed he had the magic way to do everything. I was conscious that my status as founder and owner didn't necessarily mean I knew how to lead.

So, I sought out people who, as far as I could tell, knew how to lead. As mentioned previously, over that ten-year period, I hired four different leaders. But with each one, I noticed that they would work in alignment with me for a short period of time and then begin to chart a new path for the company.

It was difficult because I liked each of them. Ultimately, though, we were not on the same page about vision. In fact, we weren't even in the same book.

I had such low confidence that I believed for a long time that everyone else had the right answers. I allowed my lack of education and experience to render my passion and vision unviable, leaving me with the belief that I had very little to offer. It took four failures of leadership by four different people to evict my low confidence and invite me into a new belief. It was *me*—with my passion, my vision, my competencies, and, according to the outside world, my lack of credentials—who should be leading the company. My lack of formal leadership experience did not disqualify the strengths I brought to the table.

Maybe you have experience with shame too. It's a compelling feeling, and it has affected many of my decisions over the years. My lack of credentials was highlighted one day when the magazine *Who's Who* gave me a call at work. They asked me some questions about my revenue and my accomplishments, and I was happy to answer. But when they asked me about my educational background, I froze. To this day, I can't remember whether I told them the truth or backed out of the conversation altogether. The truth is that I barely graduated high school and have two years of community college and no degree. I could not fully accept this reality without shame until I saw that my company was in danger of failing without my full, unapologetic contribution of leadership. It was OK to be me. In fact, my company needed me to be me.

It became obvious that I needed to take back leadership of my company.

This realization connected back to everything I had learned about embracing weaknesses. **I had discovered in my personal life that my dyslexia and learning challenges were not disqualifications. They gave me years of experience learning to deal with struggle. They taught me grit. I became familiar with—even comfortable with—failure. This allowed me to take risks in business because I wasn't paralyzed by a fear of failing. Failing was an acceptable outcome and worth the risk. I understood that my lack of formal business credentials was not a barrier to effective leadership.** My lived experience and intentions were the qualifications that mattered most. The brain of this organizational body needed to be me—not because I was perfect or all-knowing, but because I was the one who carried the clearest vision of what SnapCab was meant to be.

A NEW BEGINNING

After guiding our US company back to a healthy place, I felt a clarity and an assurance that I had never felt before. **This was not a matter of deciding to believe in myself but rather a matter of deciding to accept the gifts I had been given as a leader.** I started to see that my low confidence could have been causing harm to the company, that by thinking so poorly of myself, I might have been impeding the inspiration I had been given to contribute. Now I could make good use of my inspiration, releasing my attachment to credentials, trusting instead my passion for SnapCab's success to inform the vision for the company. My vision didn't always make sense to others—it didn't even always make sense to me right away—but whenever I followed it, things worked out. I stopped spending so much energy thinking of myself in a negative or positive light and instead got focused on what the universe was asking me to do.

Over the next three years, I worked with the Canadian management team to develop and manufacture our new custom privacy pod solution: SnapCab Workspace. This new offering included several pod layouts for individuals or groups of up to six people to meet in quiet, mobile, and flexible working spaces. In addition, we developed a demountable wall system that attached to the pods to create countless workspace configurations.

On the elevator side, I refocused the business back to standard, simple-to-install products and led the leadership teams in both locations to update and reimplement the DNA file system.

Finally back at the helm of my own company, things started to become clearer to both me and my team members. I started to communicate my desire to collaborate on projects for the sake of reaching a common intention, and I started to see the positive results. As a matter of fact, SnapCab was flourishing.

I don't intend to imply that the company was flourishing because of *me*. The company was flourishing because of mutual trust: The leadership team trusted my vision, asking for coaching and guidance, and I trusted their ideas and action items, which actualized our shared vision. We acted as a unit. We are but one example of a community operating with this complementary structure. One architect said, "I have many architects working under me, and they design the houses. But when they present me with the plans, I decide which of the plans are in and which of the plans are out." This owner is the steward of a shared vision for his company. It is his duty to maintain alignment between the new proposals and the established plans. Just as the body sends signals to the brain and the brain decides whether to act on those signals, it's a collaborative act. It's the same with me at SnapCab. It is my duty to safeguard our future, trusting my own gift of decision-making to carve out a path for the company to follow.

From there, I went on to further develop our vision with the leadership team through strategic planning and regular check-ins, including daily communications. The team would then communicate the vision and strategic projects to each of their departments and would provide me with daily status updates on progress. I would also provide regular video messages to staff and share them through Voxer broadcasts and the monthly all-company meeting.

The major shift I perceived was that instead of everyone coming to the table with their own versions of a vision for the company, they deferred the final decision to me. Instead of continual conflict around which market to enter, which products to develop, and which operating system to use, the team offered their input but rallied around me and gave me the final say. This way of operating stood in contrast to the way the company had operated in the years prior. Let's use the conversation between the stomach and the brain as an analogy. The stomach sends hunger pains to the brain and says, "We're hungry and tired. We should eat!" But the brain may put a hold on that request, understanding that the body has already consumed enough calories for the day and that energy can be regained with some light exercise. In response, the brain might say, "Hold on, I understand that we're feeling hungry, but let's drink some water and go for a walk instead." In this way, the brain receives feedback (the need) from the stomach, but filters it against the person's goal to be healthier—the direction.

Ultimately, with improved alignment came improved relation-ships, improved time management, and improved results. Everyone seemed happier. We all shared the feeling that SnapCab was about to take off again.

OUR PIVOT TO PANDEMIC PODS

We were in for a rude awakening. On March 11, 2020, SnapCab, along with virtually every other business in the world, was forced to press pause because of the global COVID-19 pandemic.

We were all forced to spread out and stay apart. It was a very tough situation, especially at first, when we didn't know how to stay open or whether we could even stay in business.

Plus, the products that SnapCab had been manufacturing were focused on keeping people together in small spaces—the exact opposite of what the world was being told to do.

On March 20, Prime Minister Justin Trudeau called upon Canadian companies, specifically manufacturers, to help in providing medical supplies and equipment in support of keeping people safe during the pandemic. Through this address, I realized that SnapCab had the capability to design and manufacture medical testing pods that could be used by healthcare workers to keep them safe.

We started connecting with local medical experts for advice and guidance, since we had no background in the medical field. We just knew we wanted to help. SnapCab quickly got to work designing and developing several prototypes for medical testing pods. We worked with the global architecture, engineering, and design firm Cannon-Design to further develop the product.

SnapCab's focus on being useful didn't end there. With much of the office-bound workforce now working from home, we took two of our larger pod layouts—originally designed as collaboration spaces—and redesigned them into one-person office pod solutions.

The team also developed a pod solution with a reduced footprint that allowed it to fit in smaller areas—such as residential spaces—and a one-person pod that was optimized for video conferencing. Additionally, SnapCab introduced a solution that allowed two people to safely have face-to-face conversations. The design included a glass partition and separate HEPA (high-efficiency particulate air) filters to provide a safe place for mask-free interactions.

Interestingly, this last solution received positive attention in the media and was coined the "God Pod" by *The Globe and Mail*, CTV News, and other international media for its use in a church in Ottawa.

This pivot during the pandemic is perhaps the clearest demonstration yet of what it means to focus on usefulness over profit. **We didn't ask, "What can we sell?" We asked, "What do people need right now, and how can our existing capabilities serve that need?"** When the world was in pain, we responded by adapting to serve that need. We weren't thinking about awards or recognition. We were thinking about how to be useful to our fellow human beings.

To our surprise, the customized mobile medical pod we designed in response to the pandemic, along with several other SnapCab Workspace layouts, started receiving local, national, and international attention.

Export Development Canada produced a commercial about the new medical pods. *Business Insider* featured SnapCab in its publication, highlighting each of the new custom privacy pods SnapCab had introduced throughout that year. SnapCab was recognized by *Fast Company's* 2021 World Changing Ideas Awards for its isolation and medical testing pods.

Honestly, we were shocked at the degree of recognition that our pods were receiving. What we did see was that we had had an intention when designing these pods: During the pandemic, we wanted to focus on what we could do to help. **We wanted to be useful to our fellow human beings.** To witness others taking note of our efforts and praising them was both surprising and rewarding, especially considering that we had only entered the pod market about four years earlier.

From the beginning of our pod journey, the team and I did not try to develop office pods that would compete with other pod companies or with what was already available on the market. Instead, with caring at the core and usefulness in mind, we used our strengths from the elevator industry and adapted them for what we felt people truly needed. That decision appeared to be what the market had wanted as well.

We were busier on the Workspace side than ever before. But things were running smoothly because our systems and processes were improving, as was our communication. There were always turnbacks to learn from, but we were moving in the right direction. If you were to look at SnapCab like a human body, a practice I was beginning to lean into, the leaders of all body parts (the department managers) were clearly communicating with the head (the CEO), and the head was communicating its vision with the body. The body was working beautifully because each part was contributing its gifts to the whole.

SUPPORTING MY LEADERSHIP TEAM

My daughter Carla, SnapCab's Director of Pod Architecture and Design at the time, had led the pod aesthetics and booth design for NeoCon. It had been her vision, with the help of the art and manufacturing teams, that led to SnapCab being awarded gold in the Work Pods category. Carla has an undeniable gift for interior design. I had understood her vision for our booth, and she had understood my vision for the company. Her vision was in alignment with mine, so I had stepped out of her way. This is a great example of accountability, something we will discuss more when we cover **RACI** (Responsible,

Accountable, Consulted, and Informed). This experience prompted my desire to support other leaders in their decision-making, provided there was alignment with the overall vision.

Just because there's an orchestra leader doesn't mean the leader is responsible for all of the music. I could see that Carla had a talent beyond mine. By using her autonomy, while maintaining alignment with the overall vision, she brought SnapCab to the next level. A higher level of public awareness and recognition paved the way for more pods to make their way to more customers. In my view, the more customers served, the higher the value of usefulness.

THE SNAPCAB WAY: PURPOSE THEN PROFITS

After thirty-eight years in business, learning and growing while making many mistakes and using them as fuel for change, it was clear that making caring and usefulness the top priorities had started to yield a greater and greater degree of attention. The company was able to succeed in attracting that attention when we weren't focused on money or being successful. In other words, the accolades were the by-products, not the purpose. In more recent years, we have been grateful for continued recognition from the interior design industry. Our hope is that an elevated awareness of these pods will lead to providing our customers with a product that enhances their lives at home, at work, or in a public setting. We intend to create communities of usefulness—both on our own shop floor and in every office with its own useful purpose to bring to life.

Because of our background in the elevator industry, where every elevator cab is a different size, we understand that we can make every pod a custom size with any material. Stone, wood, veneer, glass, metals, plastic laminates, and more. Our ability to customize pod size, material, and layout puts us in a unique position in the market. This design flexibility is unmatched in the industry. No other company offers all of these options in conjunction with high quality. We maximize usefulness by giving customers exactly what they need.

This journey—from nearly falling apart to winning international awards—demonstrated that **when foundational systems are clear and accessible, when leadership provides vision and departments work in harmony, when problems are addressed openly, and when communication keeps information flowing, that's when extraordinary things become possible**. But to understand how to build and maintain this organizational health, we need to look more closely at the specific systems that make up a Human Business.

Model Your Business After the Human Form: Part 2

I find using the human body as a metaphor is a wonderful and thorough way to represent a business.

Here's what I've come to understand: Everyone is in their own body, right? Just sit and listen to it. *Exist* in it. Are you aware of your lungs breathing in new oxygen and expelling carbon dioxide? Are you consciously aware of your ears hearing? **All of these separate body parts are functioning as part of one system in harmony.** Is this not exactly how all the departments of a healthy business function?

SnapCab is a body with component parts. Instead of organ systems, it has departments. Instead of cells, it has individual human beings. Instead of DNA, it has shared values, principles, and a company purpose or intention. Our business, SnapCab, has its own unique purpose or *use*, while other organizational bodies have their own distinct uses. Some business communities are focused on a love of helping others, while others are focused on a love of serving themselves. This group purpose informs identity, and identity shapes the culture of the company. This picture of a body, with each organ system working for a common purpose, is helpful in understanding why

SnapCab was thriving when it was thriving and why SnapCab was failing when it was failing. The cells of its body were either working in alignment with the overall company vision, or they weren't.

When a body functions properly, you don't notice the individual organs—you experience health. The same is true for organizations. When the critical systems work together, employees experience purpose, customers receive value, and leaders can focus on vision rather than firefighting.

For each body system, three questions reveal whether that system is serving your organization well:

1. **Do the necessary systems exist in my organization?** If not, you're operating without vital organs. For example, do you have employee development meetings? If not, then you are missing an endocrine system.

2. **Is this system aligned with our stated purpose?** A system may exist, but it could work against you if it's misaligned.

3. **Is this system communicating with other systems?** Isolated organs lead to organizational disease, just as they do in the body.

THE HEART: PURPOSE AND MOTIVATION

One of the first organs we develop in the womb is the heart. Culturally, the heart is seen as the home of love and caring. The physical heart pumps life-giving blood to every cell. When it comes to business, an entrepreneur needs to first care about starting the business before they can begin to grow it. In a body and in a business, the heart must come first and continue to support the entirety of the business's life. We can live without many parts of our body; we can't live without a heart.

Create a foundation of caring is the first principle in this book for a reason. We as human beings aren't energized unless we feel cared for. If we don't feel cared for, we will likely struggle to get out of bed in the morning. But creating a caring environment is not one person's job. Each of us has a responsibility to nurture the kind of environment we seek. To find care, we can contribute care. Without these individual efforts to express warmth, our company culture would grow cold. The result would be a community without a heart.

HEART ALIGNMENT

The story of Jon Kerr turning down a raise to ensure the company first made a profit is an excellent example of someone working in alignment with the heart. Jon cared more about the company being successful than his immediate personal financial gain.

Sahiza Hossenbaccus, our company president in both the US and Canada, is yet another SnapCab leader whose actions have aligned with the good of the whole since her start with the company in 2018. Sahiza, whose background is not in manufacturing but in finance, has the courage to tell me where I am not helpful to the team; she's a truth speaker. She leans into the hard questions for the sake of the whole. She also has the humility to defer to my strengths as a steward of the vision for SnapCab. She uses her financial acumen to care for the company and for the employees. Never having asked for a promotion, Sahiza stepped from CFO into the role of general manager in 2019 and then into the role of president in 2023. After a meeting with her in early 2024, a vendor of SnapCab was so impressed with SnapCab's values and Sahiza's integrity that they dropped their price. Sahiza has the trust of those whose lives she touches, including mine.

In another example of heart alignment, Joe Danko, who later became my chief operating officer, recruited his dad to come into the factory late one night to fix a gang saw that had stopped working. Joe, setting aside convenience or any demand for credit, showed up to do what was needed.

HEART MISALIGNMENT

When SnapCab began to implement Lean philosophies, one skilled craftsman was unhappy because he was quite experienced and couldn't understand why simple systems and processes should be developed so that everyone could do the work. He figured that only the people who were smart and skilled enough should be considered valuable team members. He chose to hold information hostage from others by keeping it all in his head. He became a bottleneck for company growth because he was only interested in his own growth, not the team's. Finally, after years of resistance to working in a community, he was released to find a place better suited to him. This place turned out to be a prestigious museum that employed our former employee to create unique museum displays, a job description much better suited to a person with a love of independence and expertise.

THE BRAIN: LEADERSHIP AND VISION

The human brain is the leader because it orchestrates everything that needs to be done for the body to stay alive and to thrive. In the Human Business, the brain is the CEO, with the help of the leadership team. The CEO carries the vision and makes the final, informed decision about what actions the body will take.

Virtually every action the body takes has been processed through the brain. If it hasn't been processed by the brain, the body is misaligned, which then leads to problems.

The brain determines where the body should go—which markets to serve, which products to develop, and what success means beyond quarterly earnings. It ensures all the parts work together toward this vision, preventing departments from pursuing conflicting goals like feet moving in opposite directions. The brain receives information from throughout the body and makes decisions based on the complete picture rather than any single part's perspective.

It may be difficult for some to understand why this would happen. One senior manager pointed out to me a common belief among employees that opened my eyes. He said that employees believe that if you need to go to your manager to ask questions or check in, it means you don't really know how to do your job. Additionally, if you do understand your job, you are allowed to work independently without regular communication with your manager.

Let's bring this line of thinking back to the human body analogy. Can you imagine if actions by our hands weren't the result of communication with our brains? How would our hands be able to keep our bodies performing tasks and staying out of harm's way without listening to the signals sent down from the brain? None of this would make sense. It's not a bad thing to make a big change if everyone is on the same page and moving in the same direction. But if the company CEO is not aware of the change or on board with it, the brain has been separated from the body, and the shared vision for the community may be compromised.

BRAIN ALIGNMENT

SnapCab began thriving again in 2018 because I was becoming clearer on what was and wasn't working for SnapCab. I chose to take back leadership and communicate my vision to my leadership team. They expressed respect for my values, philosophy, and judgment. The team chose to help me reach for the vision instead of working against me.

Along with providing the company vision, Cheryl and I have assumed the risk. It was riskiest when the company was moving in many different directions and pulling SnapCab's aim away from its primary purpose.

Luckily, as the sole shareholders of SnapCab, we are uniquely empowered to exert influence in the company. My own interest is in focusing on useful service over profit. The focus should be on what's useful to the customers and employees. I believe when you focus on usefulness, there are more benefits for everyone, and the money will come in service to usefulness. To be clear, money is essential for fueling the activity of the business. But money must serve a higher purpose.

Now that other SnapCab team members are on board with this thinking, we are moving more swiftly and intentionally to attract new team members to sustain our two communities of usefulness in the US and Canada.

BRAIN MISALIGNMENT

At one point, two team members were researching and pushing to implement a new enterprise resource planning (ERP) system. Prior to this, I had explored and researched ERP systems multiple times, and through this experience, in addition to working with consultants, I found that an extensive ERP system was not the right fit for SnapCab. I wanted to keep SnapCab systems and processes as simple as possible by using what was proven by experience to be more accessible to all: a visual management system with magnets on whiteboards.

One day, I discovered that one team member, with the other's guidance, had built an entire material tracking system that had taken him over a year to complete. Stunned, I reviewed the project and quickly realized they had created from scratch a system that SnapCab's finance software already had the ability to do. The finance department and I had known that this material tracking system was available. We had consciously chosen not to use it because it wasn't the right fit for SnapCab's needs. (Since then, SnapCab has used a hybrid approach by using purchased software in combination with organic processes built by the SnapCab team.) This elaborate new system built by two employees was a major waste of resources and could have been prevented if the project had been appropriately communicated to the brain and reviewed by it.

While painful, this was an excellent example of the importance of starting anything new with a napkin sketch. At SnapCab, if a team member has an idea or wants to create a prototype, they are encouraged to create a napkin sketch—**a quick, simple note and drawing to informally present the idea to their manager**. The napkin sketch process takes minutes to complete instead of hours or days (or a year, as was the case with the new materials system).

Furthermore, it avoids the time required to polish an idea that may not be in the company's best

interest. If leadership approves the initial napkin sketch because the idea is in alignment with the whole, a prototype can be made, or next steps can be taken. The body can take action in confidence, having received the brain's affirmative support.

THE BRAIN–BODY BALANCE: AVOIDING MICROMANAGEMENT

Some people worry that requiring the brain's involvement in decisions leads to micromanagement. However, alignment avoids micromanagement.

The brain provides vision: Where are we going? It sets boundaries: What's in scope and what's out? It allocates resources: What support do you need? And it establishes checkpoints: When should we review progress? Within these parameters, the hands of the organization work with considerable freedom. Creativity and innovation happen every day at SnapCab.

If micromanagement is a recurring complaint in your organization, check a few things. First, is the vision clear, or do people have to guess what leadership wants? Second, does the brain regularly share the *why* behind decisions? Third, does the body part have the skills needed for autonomy? And fourth, is the person actually aligned with the vision, or are they unknowingly at odds with it?

THE CELLULAR SYSTEM: YOUR FOUNDATIONAL OPERATING PRINCIPLES

The cellular system is the foundational system in the human body. A cell is the smallest unit of life. Cells are the building blocks of everything from tissues to organs to organ systems. **Within each cell's nucleus is DNA, a set of instructions that allow the cell to know exactly what it's a part of and what it's supposed to do.**

Wouldn't it be amazing if every person at your organization considered themselves a cell that worked together with others to form a whole body? Each cell would have access to a DNA system, which, practically speaking, includes everything an employee would need to know about their job as it relates to the company, including operating instructions, SOPs, and organizational charts.

DNA COMPONENTS

While the DNA system is our operations manual, a vital practical resource for each of our employees, **the term** DNA **also indicates what binds us together at the deepest level**: shared intentions, shared values, and shared principles. Ideally, everyone in every role would know what's expected of them and how to go about fulfilling their role, as well as how their role fits in with the entire body. So, the manufacturing arm of the body, for example, would have the shared intention to make the products that go out the door; and the HR department would have the shared intention to hire the people who make the products go out the door. All people in both departments would invest in practicing kindness, practicing authenticity, and practicing usefulness. And all people in both departments would subscribe to the five principles that constitute a healthy Human Business.

COMPANY INTENTION

Create communities of usefulness. This is the place to start with every individual human being in a given community. If each one wants to work for the same purpose, there is a chance of harmony.

CORE VALUES

Be kind. Be authentic. Be useful. Without these shared values, a person will never find a happy, useful life in a Human Business.

> **PRINCIPLES**
> 1. Create a foundation of caring.
> 2. Understand your ruling love.
> 3. Focus on being useful.
> 4. Embrace problems and weaknesses.
> 5. Model your business after the human form.

Ultimately, misalignment in a business occurs when there isn't a clear understanding of each cell's role in the body. Without a clear understanding, there is room for confusion, misinterpretation, and error.

Ironically, it is our human experience that can contribute to conflict in a Human Business. Every person brings their unique personality, skills, thoughts, and feelings to the workplace. Naturally, most of us crave autonomy. We tend to like and believe our own thoughts, feelings, and ideas. This can get tricky, though, when we are working with other people who also like and believe in their own thoughts and feelings.

But if we're a part of a Human Business, we have to be clear with ourselves: Each of us, like a fractal, is one cell in an entire system of cells that runs a body. Each cell comes with DNA that includes clear instructions and a picture of what the entire body is trying to achieve.

Each of us—including me—has to be clear on who is leading the company. In the case of SnapCab, I am the primary steward of the company vision. The workers—the cells in this particular body of SnapCab—must be clear on whether they want to accept that leadership and accept the company intention. If they don't accept the leadership and intention, it's important for them to stop and reflect on their work and their role in it. It's important for them to consider whether they even want to continue working for the company.

On the other hand, if they decide that they do accept the company leadership, they must be clear on how they can work with their colleagues to support the company intention. If workers don't know how to contribute their support, managers must be available to answer these questions. Asking managers for guidance is critical, if humbling, since a Human Business requires constant communication to maintain alignment of purpose.

CELLULAR SYSTEM ALIGNMENT

Some people may start working at SnapCab with no clear role or title. But like a cell in a human body, they act as one part of the whole when placed into the area where they can be the most useful. They just want to contribute to the bigger picture.

When an employee leaves, their duties are picked up quickly by internal team members because their job description, duties, and training materials are simple to access in the DNA system. Two separate cells could be informed by the same genetic instructions, the DNA.

This is the power of institutional knowledge over head knowledge. When expertise lives only in one person's head, that person becomes a bottleneck. When knowledge is systematized in the DNA, the organization can adapt and grow.

CELLULAR SYSTEM MISALIGNMENT

In a sales department meeting, team members were rating priorities for various projects. One sales member, who oversaw East Coast sales, gave low ratings to projects belonging to the team member in charge of West Coast sales. If he had viewed sales as an organ system where each cell works together to make the body function, he would have rated West Coast projects with the same importance as his own territory.

This experience revealed a fundamental misalignment. These weren't cells working toward a common purpose—they were competitors working against each other. As a result, we restructured entirely, renaming sales associates as customer experience liaisons and shifting from chasing new clients to serving existing ones who had reached out to us.

The lesson: When cells compete rather than cooperate, you don't have an organizational body—you have a collection of separate organisms fighting for resources.

RACI: ORGANIZING CELLULAR ROLES

Each team member should have a clear job description, management structure, and understanding of who exactly their customer is. In thinking about the brain leading our organization and various body cells supporting the brain, a useful resource is the responsibility assignment matrix known as RACI. An organizational tool that became popular in the 1970s for department, project, and SOP management, RACI helps people on a team understand who should be *responsible, accountable, consulted, and informed.*

Each of us has someone or something we are working for: a primary customer. In my case, as CEO, my primary customer is the market. For the operations team, the customer is the operations manager. For the operations manager, the customer is the CEO. Everyone in a Human Business has a customer, and it's not always the person buying the company's product.

More broadly speaking, I aspire to be a servant leader, making all the employees at SnapCab my customers. For instance, I have a responsibility to provide the employees with a caring workplace. As an employer, my employees are my customers; as an entrepreneur, the market is my customer.

At SnapCab, our DNA system is both practical and philosophical. Practically, it's a digital repository containing job descriptions and role expectations, SOPs, training materials and development paths, organizational charts showing how roles interconnect, and decision-making frameworks such as RACI. Philosophically, it contains our values—the why behind the what (the mission and vision). This combination ensures that people don't just know what to do; they understand why it matters and how their role connects to the whole.

Here are the definitions for each role:

- **Responsible:** the person/people who perform a task or activity

- **Accountable:** the decision-maker who assigns tasks to those responsible (this is where the buck stops, as there can only be one accountable person for a given task or activity)

- **Consulted:** the person/people who should be asked before proceeding because they have expertise or information that needs to be considered

- **Informed:** the person/people who are told about the project when everything is finished

For more on how SnapCab uses RACI, follow the *A Human Business* YouTube channel.

THE NERVOUS SYSTEM

The physiology of the human nervous system can help us see how the organs of a company talk to each other. First, there's the central nervous system—our brain and spinal cord. Then there's the peripheral nervous system—all our other nerves. The brain sends and receives messages via the spine to the nerves of the body. So, if we think of company leadership as the brain, our leadership team is constantly communicating signals through the nerves of the spinal column to the body of the company—to its limbs, organs, tissues, and cells.

In your organization, managers are the nervous system. They carry messages from leadership (the brain) to employees (the body) and back again. When the nervous system fails, the body can't coordinate. You get paralysis, confusion, or random movements that don't serve the whole.

The nervous system has four critical functions. First, it facilitates two-way communication. Information flows from brain to body (that's your instructions) and from body to brain (that's your feedback). Managers facilitate both directions. Second, it prioritizes signals. Not every signal needs immediate attention. The nervous system filters: What's routine? What's concerning? What's urgent? Third, it manages pain response. When something goes wrong, nerves communicate the location and intensity of pain, allowing an appropriate response. In business, this is your problem-reporting system. And fourth, it coordinates action. Nerves ensure different body parts move together. Managers ensure departments work in coordination, not isolation.

THE GEMBA: YOUR ORGANIZATIONAL PAIN RESPONSE

At SnapCab, our nervous system relies heavily on the *Gemba*, a Japanese word for "actual place." We introduced this tool in the chapter called "Principle 4: Embrace Problems and Weaknesses." In this chapter, we will elaborate further on this essential tool.

Gemba is practiced on a series of simple, physical boards located in places where the work is actually done. On these boards, all team members have the opportunity to log issues with sticky notes to signal that something is going wrong. With that vital information, managers, along with employees, can determine whether the problem will cause further damage and if they should develop a countermeasure.

Before SnapCab's implementation of the Gemba, the leadership team would have daily sit-down meetings in the conference room to discuss turnbacks that were tracked in an invisible electronic system. The turnbacks weren't tracked in a simple way, and issues were not always addressed effectively. The Gemba, a physical tool, provides a clear, obvious method of tracking that all employees can easily access—and use.

Although the Gemba board isn't the place to come up with solutions, it is the place to bring issues to light. It is then management's job to act as the nerves to make sure that the learning that comes to light at the Gemba board is communicated to other parts of the organization that need to be consulted and informed. What triggers the nerves into action? Let's look to the body for answers.

In a Human Business, it is the managers who can check the Gemba board for reports of duration and intensity of a particular issue. Specifically, the Gemba board allows the managers to see how many times a problem has occurred and how much time was wasted in dealing with the turnback. It is with these specific details in mind that they filter their communication according to priority. The more pain the team feels, the faster a manager acts to carry the information to the brain for consultation.

Typically, the countermeasure for a turnback is developed by a team of employees, selected by the manager, who collaborate and develop an improvement together. This collaborative activity, mentioned earlier in the book, is called a *kaizen*. Originating from Japan, this word means "improvement" or "change for the better," with *kai* meaning "change" or "revision" and *zen* meaning "virtue" or "goodness."

Once the improvement has been determined, it is communicated to everyone involved so that the entire team can continue to work as one unit.

When it comes to maintaining a healthy business or body, it's important to deal with things promptly, as they come up. It is not advisable to report a problem, decide it's worth addressing, then wait a year to come up with a countermeasure. In a Human Business, we don't wait for an employee review to address recurring problems. We encourage ongoing two-way communication and ongoing coaching.

Coaching someone in real time and educating in real time create a great community of colleagues. If we ignore the problem, putting off the needed coaching time, we may end up losing people. We have been guilty of this in the past, but we are committed to doing better. We, as leaders, are committed to addressing problems now—not later—offering our attention to both people and the issues that disrupt the harmony of their work.

Real-time coaching is important, but pre-scheduled meetings are key too. To maintain healthy relationships, managers can schedule one-to-one meetings with team members to provide the type of feedback that keeps both parties clear and happy.

NERVOUS SYSTEM ALIGNMENT

When Kyle held the role of operations manager in Canada, he built rapport on the shop floor. A similar role to this is now held by Seth Lamoureux, production manager at SnapCab's Kingston location, who also builds rapport with the shop workers (in fact, all workers, including the office staff). Seth leads a daily meeting around all the Gemba boards with everyone in the factory. Each person takes the opportunity to share what is going wrong, and then various teams are assigned tasks to address problems. From there, the issues and countermeasures are communicated to the management team, ensuring shared awareness of the recent changes. Keeping managers in the loop about updates on the shop floor allows them to maintain alignment with any active strategic initiatives that are already in place across the whole company.

Seth also communicates with the executive team through daily check-ins and weekly meetings. In these sessions, he reviews metrics, discusses issues, and updates the management team on progress or new initiatives on the factory floor. Seth understands that we are operating as one organism, so he consciously connects all parts. Just like the nerves send signals to the brain, Seth alerts leadership to issues and, from there, provides the body with the brain's instructions.

NERVOUS SYSTEM MISALIGNMENT

A former area leader on the shop floor had been causing misery for his fellow team members by intimidating new recruits and spreading rumors. An active part of the nervous system, he was practicing communication with teammates, but it was not done out of goodwill. This employee told some new team members that if he trained them on how to do their job, they would have to give him a percentage of their paycheck. He also said that if they tracked their wasted time in a turnback and posted it to the Gemba—something that is encouraged at SnapCab—the time would be taken out of their pay. These comments were false and destructive to the company culture.

Unfortunately, the issues with this employee were initially unknown to upper management, and it took some time for the new team members to speak up. Finally, one day, a new recruit asked the shop foreman how exactly his trainer, the area leader mentioned previously, would get paid for helping him learn how to do his job. "Does the money that goes to them come out of my paycheck?" he asked. That's when the shop foreman recognized the issue: The area leader had been deliberately confusing his teammates. This behavior was reported, and after multiple attempts to coach the employee to bring him into alignment with the values of the company, he was let go. At SnapCab, it is intolerable for one person to make it difficult for another person to come to work.

This employee did not respect new people. He told management directly that it was skills and experience that were most important to him. He subscribed to a system based on seniority, one in which he could dominate and intimidate the ones who were vulnerable. But this employee concealed the bullying behavior from his own manager. His unwillingness to tell the truth created a disconnect in the line of communication between the nerves of the peripheral nervous system and those of the central nervous system.

SnapCab is a merit-based company, different from a company where employee growth is based on seniority. If you're a team member who has worked for SnapCab for a long period of time, our hope is that you merit more responsibility because of the experiences you have gained, not simply the time spent at work. Quality of experience is more important than quantity of experience.

If you ask us about our hiring priorities, we are clear that it is more important for our employees to be a cultural fit than it is for them to come to us with any special training in their craft. Aptitude is also important, since we want to give people the opportunity to exercise their existing strengths. Ultimately, experience can be gained with a willing attitude and good aptitude, but a willing attitude and good aptitude cannot be gained with experience.

Employees are encouraged to report any and all problems they are having to make way for change and improvement. I want everyone to feel safe and supported at work. **Everyone who comes to work has the right to be approached with kindness and treated with dignity.**

THE IMMUNE SYSTEM: PROTECTING YOUR CULTURE

As you know, the immune system acts as the body's main defender, protecting against viruses and bacteria that can make it sick.

Quite a number of systems at SnapCab function like the immune system, including the PIP. A **PIP** is given to any employee who continues to show that they are out of alignment with the company's values and principles. An employee's misaligned behavior is actually a *manager's* turnback and, therefore, an opportunity for the manager to repair what is not working. It is an opportunity for the manager to offer training opportunities and invite reconciliation. A customized, ninety-day PIP plan records the issues and highlights training opportunities using resources such as this book, videos such as our YouTube channel (*A Human Business*), and other books. A future reassessment may include an agreement to review additional material that the manager deems useful to the employee.

There is a difference between performance and personal culture alignment. An employee who is getting more work out the door than their coworkers but is abrasive and demeaning to their coworkers may think that their job is secure because they believe performance equals producing. Management sees that ruining the company culture is poor performance, so they would provide a PIP. Creating an environment where everyone feels respected and cared for comes first. When the ninety-day PIP period is completed, some employees have come into alignment with the company's vision, values, and principles. Others find a job with another company that they believe will suit them better. Ultimately, if an obvious misalignment remains, the employee is transitioned out of the company. SnapCab's culture of kindness postponed our implementation of PIPs initially. Most people wanted to be kind to each other, but it led to confusion about how to handle difficult interpersonal situations. But as Brené Brown says, "Being clear is being kind."

Now we aim to first coach and lead, making use of clear direction as a means of expressing kindness. If things are still not moving in a good direction, we may institute a PIP. The hope is that with the PIP, the employee has a chance to respond and work to achieve alignment with SnapCab principles and become a productive team member. The PIP helps us avoid a discipline-oriented, fear-based culture. Our intention is to create an open, productive environment that invites a struggling person to walk the path of continuous improvement with dignity.

Joe Danko shed some light on the challenge of addressing unkind behavior in the workplace. He said that in the past, team members have confessed their hesitation to report the bad behavior of coworkers. They did not want to be seen as tattletales to management. "But it's not about tattling," Joe says. "It's about stepping up for the company culture we all want to have." Bringing an issue into the light is good for everyone. "The earlier we become aware of the misalignment, the better it is for SnapCab and the individual who could be pursuing a career elsewhere with another company."

Ideally, the person receiving the PIP gains a new understanding that they did not have originally. By accepting support, they can move into harmony and alignment with SnapCab's values and principles.

What was initially a problem can now be part of a positive alignment experience. After all, the body's immune system becomes stronger the more it is tested. Similarly, when we accept problems and weaknesses, we too have the opportunity to grow stronger. The more issues that we choose to pull into the light, the more capable the company will be—if we also choose to take positive action. That is, we can mistake-proof our systems, add additional training, document SOPs, or implement other helpful tools that enhance the company's harmony and functionality.

The book *Built to Last* by Jim Collins highlights businesses that have lasted 150 years or longer. The author says that these businesses last because they have clear belief systems that create cultures where a person either fits or doesn't fit. If they fit, they know exactly what the company stands for and work to uphold the culture. If they don't fit, the company's immune system pushes the person out, somewhat like a splinter in a body.

IMMUNE SYSTEM ALIGNMENT

One manifestation of immune system alignment is in the way we've set up the SnapCab Careers page. This page features approximately twenty minutes of videos for applicants to watch that describe SnapCab's workplace culture very carefully. We have found that the people who are a fit are very excited about the video content and eager to join the SnapCab community of usefulness, while the people who are not a fit will hardly get through one of the videos and be discouraged by the lengthy application process. This Careers page supports SnapCab's immune system because it acts as a filter for applicants before they become members of the SnapCab team.

IMMUNE SYSTEM MISALIGNMENT

A very experienced person out on the manufacturing floor was misaligned with the company culture; he felt SnapCab should only be hiring the most skilled people and that people who were hired more for cultural fit were a problem for the company.

This individual would complain to management about the lack of training the new people had. Being a senior person, he was in the perfect position to offer training and coaching to new employees. Instead, he would shame and laugh at them for their lack of knowledge.

Over the years, our experience has been that those who are a strong cultural fit are eager to work as part of a team and are the fastest to be trained. They can become our most productive employees because they are doing what they want to do. They are doing what they love.

The employee who had been mistreating the new workers was given a PIP, and during the time the PIP was in place, his attitude did not change.

The employee resigned from SnapCab after finding employment with another company. Some months later, this employee reached out to see if he could be rehired. Thanks to the PIP process and the clarity of principles outlined in this book, his manager was very clear that he was not a fit at SnapCab. He was not rehired.

PUTTING IT ALL TOGETHER: THE INTEGRATED BODY

These systems don't operate independently—they function as an integrated whole. The heart pumps the needed nutrients, caring for the entire body. The cellular system ensures everyone operates from shared DNA. The nervous system keeps all parts communicating. The immune system protects the integrity of the whole. The brain coordinates it all, based on the intended purpose of the organization.

When one system fails, others compensate—but only for a time. A body with a weak heart can survive if other organs work harder, but eventually, the strain becomes too much. An organization with poor communication can get by if the brain micromanages every decision, but this isn't sustainable. A company without clear values can muddle through if leadership constantly intervenes, but this creates exhaustion and frustration.

The goal is harmony. When all the systems work together, you experience organizational health. Employees know their purpose and feel cared for. Leadership provides a clear vision without controlling every detail. Everyone understands their role and how it connects to the whole. Information flows freely up and down. Culture protects itself through natural filtration based on an understanding of what a Human Business is.

This is what it means to model your business after the human form. Not a rigid hierarchy where the brain dominates and the body blindly obeys. Not a flat structure where every cell does whatever it wants. But an integrated organism where every part knows its function, communicates with other parts, and works toward a shared purpose.

Your business is already a body—the question is whether it's a healthy one. Use these systems as your diagnostic framework. Assess each one honestly. Strengthen the weak systems. Ensure they're communicating with each other. And remember: Organizational health, like physical health, requires ongoing attention. You don't exercise once to strengthen your heart and think you have attained health.

The human form gives us a model not just for structure but for continuous care. Bodies need rest, nourishment, exercise, and healing. So do organizations. The practices I've described—the assessments, the strengthening protocols, the alignment examples—aren't one-time projects. They're ongoing rhythms of organizational life.

When you embrace this model, you're choosing to see your business as a living thing. And living things grow, adapt, learn, and sometimes struggle. That's not failure; that's the way of growth. The question isn't whether your organizational body will face challenges. The question is whether you have the systems in place to recognize those challenges early, respond appropriately, and emerge stronger.

This is the promise of the human form: not perfection but resilience. Not control but coordination. When you model your business after the human body, you create space for people to be fully human at work—complex, interconnected, purposeful, and alive.

CONCLUSION

*The more one forgets himself—by giving himself to
a cause to serve or another person to love—the more
human he is and the more he actualizes himself.*
—VIKTOR FRANKL

The current convention of business—the one that prioritizes profit above all else—damages our ability to work in healthy, meaningful ways. The cultural norms that tell us to be hard and ruthless take away from our sense of humanity and purpose, creating cold working environments that are not only harmful to our mental health and well-being but undermine a company's chances of success.

This book introduces a new way of doing business—one that supports our people and our profits by focusing on what is *useful* to our customers. We've shown how the five key principles of the Human Business model can turn businesses into incredible communities—places that not only improve services and products but also make a real difference in people's lives. However, if you only take away one thing from this book, take away this: It starts with caring.

1. CREATE A FOUNDATION OF CARING

There's a reason "create a foundation of caring" is the first principle of a Human Business. A caring environment is essential for both individual and organizational success. When people feel valued and supported, they thrive. They're more motivated, more creative, and more resilient. Conversely, a lack of care can lead to decreased morale, lower productivity, and higher turnover. By prioritizing care, you unlock the full potential of your team. They'll be more willing to embrace challenges, adapt to change, and deliver exceptional results.

2. UNDERSTAND YOUR RULING LOVE

Understanding your ruling love is crucial for finding fulfilling work. When you align your passions with your career, you'll experience increased energy, motivation, and productivity. This not only benefits you but also makes you an invaluable asset to your company.

3. FOCUS ON BEING USEFUL

True usefulness comes from recognizing a need and utilizing your unique talents to address it. It's doing something that benefits others and not just yourself. The key is to identify work that truly excites and energizes you. By aligning your passions with your purpose, you can create meaningful impact and find lasting fulfillment. As your needs and passions change, so too does your primary source of energy and motivation. If you feel the need to shift your focus to be more useful, don't hesitate! Embrace the evolving nature of your ruling love and use its power to drive your useful actions. By understanding the elements that ignite your passion, you can channel that energy into meaningful work.

4. EMBRACE PROBLEMS AND WEAKNESSES

Think about your life. If you're feeling hopeless and you're struggling—that's OK. This is your path to growth. Problems aren't to be avoided; they're opportunities that are necessary. Just like going to the gym—you go to stretch and tear your muscle so you can grow new muscle. The problems are creating a situation where you are stretched and torn so you can grow as a person. No problems, no growth. But, you don't have to go to the gym to get problems. The gym comes to you—the problems will come find you! Ignoring them only compounds them, leading to negative consequences for ourselves and those around us. Instead, let's view problems as avenues for improvement. Embracing challenges with a growth mindset allows us to learn and adapt. Not only that, sharing our failures fosters stronger connections with others. By acknowledging our limitations and seeking support, we create a more empathetic and understanding community.

Welcome to a lifetime of problems!

5. MODEL YOUR BUSINESS AFTER THE HUMAN FORM

The human body provides a powerful metaphor for understanding the interconnectedness of a business and aligning employees with their roles and responsibilities within the company. Just as a healthy body relies on the harmonious function of its various organs, a thriving business depends on the collaborative efforts of its team members. By adopting this perspective, we can foster a culture of cooperation and mutual support. Each individual plays a vital role in the overall health and success of the organization, and when we work together seamlessly, we can achieve extraordinary results. Most importantly, it encourages a sense of belonging and shared purpose, inspiring everyone to contribute their unique strengths to the collective goal.

My work has taught me that it's not only OK to be human; it's the whole purpose, the intended design.

What we can do now is go to work being ourselves, doing what we love to do. As ourselves, we can contribute what is ours to give in order to bring our shared intention to life. We can each do our part to grow communities of usefulness.

My hope is that the chapters of this book have illustrated, for your benefit, an alternate reality in which work is a place we want to be, a place to be who we are—each of us a vital cell in a body of cells working to move a common intention to useful action.

If your energy is bubbling and you're wondering what you can do next, take what you've learned in this book and put it to good use. Bring your team together and make a plan to transform your workplace into a community of usefulness.

A community of people who contribute what they love, need each other, accept and grow from problems, and create maximum value for your customers.

I can't think of a better way to build a life of purpose.

A Message to the SnapCab Community and Beyond

This isn't the end—it's a moment in an ongoing journey. As I write from my home on Wolfe Island, watching the sun rise over the St. Lawrence River, I reflect on the life I've been given.

The secret is simple:

It's not about you. It's about what you can contribute.

When you begin to see your work as a way to serve others, something shifts. You realize that you don't have to do it all on your own. You begin to rely on the people around you—your team, your community—and together, you build something far greater than any one person could build alone.

If you've ever wondered how to become a more effective leader, how to produce meaningful work, or how to build a business that truly matters—know that it requires authenticity and kindness. When you're honest about your strengths and your weaknesses, when you show appreciation and care for others, and when your intention is to be useful to the world, people will want to work with you.

I've dreamed of offering the SnapCab team—and anyone searching for a more meaningful way to work—a clear and comprehensive model for what I call a Human Business. This model is more than a framework; it's a way of life. It brings clarity, reduces fear, and enhances joy.

At the heart of our model is an analogy: the human body. Every person in the organization is a cell—correlating to a brain, heart, or eye cell—and each has a role in serving the whole. Leadership isn't about ruling; it's about serving. The doers are the reason we exist, and leaders must support them with tools, information, and encouragement. When we operate as one organism, united by a shared intention to serve usefully, we move swiftly and harmoniously toward goals that matter.

To fellow leaders in business: As you finish this book, I invite you to begin your own next chapter.

If you've read this with interest, we already share a spiritual community. You want to reprioritize values—subordinating knowledge to love, profit to service, and individual success to community happiness. These values are universal:

Be kind. Be authentic. Be useful.

If your leadership is failing, good. If your culture is eroding, don't worry. These holes are outlines for your priority projects. A good litmus test could be to ask yourself how a dynamic in your business would play out in the body. For example, if you are dealing with unhealthy competition between teams, that correlates with a disease process in the body. It is my hope that entrepreneurs and business owners can tap into the power of the human body model.

I invite you to tour SnapCab and meet the incredible people who make this place what it is.

I hope we connect soon and learn from each other. And I hope you find joy, meaning, and purpose in your journey.

—GLENN H. BOSTOCK

Founder and CEO, SnapCab

My love of building products has expanded into a love of building a company of people who collaborate together using our strengths of what we love to do to create useful products. We have a community of caring teammates who see each other's weaknesses as an opportunity to help each other and our problems as a way to grow together and to grow stronger.
—GLENN BOSTOCK

CONNECT

VISIT GLENNBOSTOCK.COM and sign up for our newsletter to hear about community building, upcoming speaking engagements, training opportunities, new tools and materials, and future books and videos that dive deeper into the Human Business model.

GLOSSARY

Above the Line: Thinking or acting in a way that benefits others and puts them first. Approaching scenarios or problems with curiosity, humility, and a desire to be useful without needing any credit (from *The 15 Commitments of Conscious Leadership* by Jim Dethmer).

All-Company Meeting: A way that SnapCab practices authenticity with its employees. Each month, the entire company gathers to hear the leadership team give a transparent update on the company's direction, struggles, and successes. This meeting also doubles as a monthly celebration where the company provides everyone lunch, prizes are awarded, and more.

Anniversary Video: A way that SnapCab practices kindness with its employees. A video is created for an employee to celebrate each year that they have worked with the company. The video includes congratulatory messages from their colleagues and manager and is broadcast to the whole company, so everyone can participate in congratulating and thanking the person. Anniversary videos make employees feel cared for and appreciated. They're also wonderful ways for workers to learn more about the people they work with.

Be Authentic: Being open about your strengths and weaknesses. In what ways can you be of use to your community? What are the areas that you need help with?

Be Kind: Treating everyone with support, patience, and encouragement. Doing your part to maintain a low-fear environment (we don't blame people, we blame systems). Understanding that we all work differently, approach things differently, and have different things going on in our lives.

Be Useful: Being useful isn't just about *wanting* to be useful or *knowing* how to be useful. It's about taking action. It's about blending desire and skill and then actually doing the thing.

Below the Line: Thinking or acting in a way that is coming from your ego. For example, blaming others to camouflage your own mistakes or downplaying a colleague's strengths because you feel intimidated (from *The 15 Commitments of Conscious Leadership* by Jim Dethmer).

Community of Usefulness: A group of people with a common set of values who support each other so they can provide a useful product or service to the world.

Continuous Improvement: The act of forever implementing quick and small changes to a system or process (or even yourself).

Countermeasure: A response to a **turnback**, a quick solution that leaves room for future improvements.

Customer: In **Human Business** terms, this doesn't necessarily refer to the client purchasing the product or service. Rather, the customer is anyone, inside or outside the business, you aim to **be useful** to. A customer may be your manager, your employee, a different department in your company, and so on.

DNA: A repository of company information that is accessible to all the employees. The DNA system stores all the instructions and resources that you need to do your job and for the business to function and is also a system that helps the company scale.

Employee Development Plan: A career path that is built in collaboration with an employee and their leadership team to ensure that both the individual and the company are benefiting from the time spent in employment. This career path may include growth, such as position changes or promotions, and will include training plans and materials to facilitate that growth. The plan intends to align what the employee loves to do with what the company needs to **be useful**.

Escape: When a mistake or error (**turnback**) is not captured and makes its way to the customer. Examples include giving a customer the wrong coffee order or presenting incorrect sales figures to an important client.

Fractal: A never-ending pattern, a repetition of a system into smaller and smaller parts. A **Human Business** is a fractal, in that the metaphor of the **human form** can be seen to repeat within the business, departments, and even the employees themselves. For example: A business's leadership is the "head," and all the departments that are led by it are different functioning "body parts." Now, when you observe a single department, you realize that it can exist as a human form as well, where the team lead is the "head" and the different employees function as different "body parts."

Gemba: A Japanese term meaning "the actual place." At SnapCab, Gemba boards are placed in areas of the building where the actual work is being done. Workers use these boards to report issues, **turnbacks**, and **escapes**. These boards are reviewed by the workers and leadership on a regular basis. Gemba is not a to-do list; it is a thermometer system to monitor what's not working in the company. Workers use the Gemba boards to identify repeating problems or issues and, from there, propose fixes via **kaizen** forms.

Gold: Imagine finding gold on the floor. That's the value of identifying **turnbacks**! By doing this, we uncover hidden opportunities for improvement. This helps us streamline processes, reduce costs, and ultimately enhance our products and services.

Hansei: A Japanese term referring to the practice of self-consciousness or self-awareness. It's pausing to consider your role(s) within a scenario, interaction, or environment and analyzing, with humility, the effect that your actions (or reactions) may have had. This practice helps us to identify areas of ourselves that we can improve, or amendments we need to perform.

Head Knowledge: Skills or know-how that exist purely in a worker's mind. These are not recorded or written down in any SOPs or company documents. This is a dangerous way to store useful information, because if the worker leaves the company or decides not to share with their colleagues, that knowledge will be lost.

Higher Power: Something that is outside of you and bigger than you that you believe in. It could be family, friends, a mentor, or even a favorite book. It's a place you can go to, in your mind, when you need help from your higher self to be an **above-the-line** person.

Human Business: A useful community that uses the human body as a metaphor for how its employees and departments should collaborate together.

Human Form: The limbs, organs, cells, and all other components and functions of the human body can be an excellent metaphor to help articulate an employee's role within the greater organism (body) of the company.

ILP (interlocking paneling) System: A groundbreaking, Lean solution Glenn invented in response to the need for easy-to-install elevator interior solutions. This useful system allows prefabricated horizontal panels to be stacked on top of each other, reducing installation time from four days down to one. It has a flexible design that accommodates for imperfection, and its simple design makes it easy to install.

Kaizen: A Japanese term meaning "change for the better" and referring to the incentive of **continuous improvement**. At SnapCab, we write down ideas for improvements on kaizen forms, which are then reviewed by the leadership team. The leadership team may consult with employees on their kaizen forms, and, together, they'll develop an improvement plan. Once approved, this plan will be posted on the kaizen board and assigned to an employee to complete during **improvement time**.

Lean: Originated by the Toyota Production System, Lean is a set of practices that produce value for customers by reducing delays and eliminating waste, resulting in increased quality and lower cost. The two foundational principles are respect for people and continuous improvement.

Mistake-Proof: A mechanism or method in a system or process that either makes it impossible for an error to occur or makes the error immediately obvious by stopping the system so that a fix may be implemented before proceeding.

Napkin Sketch: A quick way for workers to share improvement ideas with their managers. They are rough, informal proposals (e.g., whiteboard drawings, short videos) that focus on conveying the core idea. Napkin sketches reduce the time investment for employees, allow for faster feedback from leadership, and allow for improved team collaboration.

PIP (performance improvement plan): When an employee is presenting misaligned behavior, a PIP is used to help bring them back into alignment with the company. This is an opportunity for the employee and their leadership team to discuss responsibilities and expectations and to identify areas where the employee has not received enough support or training from their managers. A ninety-day plan is developed, during which the employee will receive training through a variety of resources (possibly including this book), and, at the end of it, they will be reassessed to see if they are still a good fit (or even *want* to be a fit) for the company.

RACI (responsible, accountable, consulted, and informed): A method of designating roles within a project or incentive. The person *accountable* oversees everything, and the success or failure of the thing is dependent on them. Those *responsible* are the ones doing the actual work, implementing changes or initiating fixes. *Consulted* people are the ones whom the *responsible* or *accountable* individuals may come to for advice or guidance. *Informed* people are the ones whom the *responsible* or *accountable* individuals will notify regarding completion or progress.

Root Cause: The fundamental reason why a **turnback** keeps happening. This method was created by Toyota Motor Corporation.

To discover the root cause of a problem, ask *why* it occurred, typically five times.

Example of the Five Whys from Ito University:

"My car has a flat tire."

Why? There is a nail in it.

Why? There were nails on the garage floor.

Why? A cardboard box of nails on a shelf broke.

Why? It got wet.

Why? There's a hole in the garage roof.

The hole in the roof is the root cause, so fixing this issue should prevent the chain of issues from happening again.

Ruling Love: A person may have many loves, but your ruling love is the one thing that all the **supporting loves** point to, the thing that gets you up in the morning. It is the deep, inexplicable desire to do one thing that lights you up, brings you joy, and allows you to experience a flow state where time seems to race by. For example: If you love training your dog, volunteering to do crafts with kids at the library, and onboarding new staff members, maybe your ruling love involves teaching.

Shadow Boxing: A **Lean** practice where an outline or cutout is placed around each tool within a station, so that it is easy to know where each tool is stored. Shadow boxing also makes it so that it's immediately known when a tool has gone missing.

Spiritual Work: Spirit refers to your thoughts and feelings. Nearly identical to **hansei**, spiritual work means observing how your *spirit* presents itself at *work*—to your colleagues—and reflecting on how you can improve it. Spiritual work is striving to incorporate **above-the-line** thinking and actions, through reflection, into your daily working routine. It's not fun working on yourself, but it's necessary to grow as a person.

Subordinate Love/Supporting Love: Activities you enjoy doing that recharge you and help you fulfill your **ruling love**. For instance, you may love having people over for a BBQ because it supports your ruling love of community.

Turnback: Anything that hinders the flow of work, big or small. These can be mistakes or errors caused by equipment failure, system failure, human error, etc. that force the work process to be *turned around* from reaching the goal or the purpose of the thing or activity. Examples include a printer running out of paper or a part being damaged. Relating to **hansei** or **spiritual work**, hurting a relationship through **below-the-line** communications, such as gossip or anger, could be considered a spiritual turnback because negative work environments hinder the flow of work.

RESOURCES

INTRODUCTION

"Forget the Paycheck, Employees Really Want a Raise in Emotional Salary" by Hannah Yardley, *Fast Company*, 2024

Traction: Get a Grip on Your Business by Gino Wickman, 2011

PRINCIPLE 1: CREATE A FOUNDATION OF CARING

The Carrot Principle: How the Best Managers Use Recognition to Engage Their People, Retain Talent, and Accelerate Performance by Adrian Gostick and Chester Elton, 2007

Delivering Happiness: A Path to Profits, Passion, and Purpose by Tony Hsieh, 2010

Love 'Em or Lose 'Em: Getting Good People to Stay by Beverly Kaye and Sharon Jordan-Evans, 2014

How to Win Friends and Influence People by Dale Carnegie, 1936

Servant Leadership: A Journey into the Nature of Legitimate Power and Greatness by Robert K. Greenleaf, 1977

PRINCIPLE 2: UNDERSTAND YOUR RULING LOVE

The Artist's Way: A Spiritual Path to Higher Creativity by Julia Cameron, 1992

First, Break All the Rules: What the World's Greatest Managers Do Differently by Marcus Buckingham and Curt Coffman, 1999

StrengthsFinder 2.0 by Tom Rath, 2007

The Well-Lived Life: A 102-Year-Old Doctor's Six Secrets to Health and Happiness at Every Age by Dr. Gladys McGarey, 2023

PRINCIPLE 3: FOCUS ON BEING USEFUL

Atomic Habits: An Easy & Proven Way to Build Good Habits & Break Bad Ones by James Clear, 2018

The Four Agreements: A Practical Guide to Personal Freedom by Don Miguel Ruiz, 1997

A New Earth: Awakening to Your Life's Purpose by Eckhart Tolle, 2005

The Speed of Trust: The One Thing That Changes Everything by Stephen M. R. Covey, 2006

Tribal Leadership: Leveraging Natural Groups to Build a Thriving Organization by David Logan, John King, and Halee Fischer-Wright, 2008

The 4 Disciplines of Execution: Achieving Your Wildly Important Goals by Chris McChesney, Sean Covey, and Jim Huling, 2012

The 15 Commitments of Conscious Leadership: A New Paradigm for Sustainable Success by Jim Dethmer, Diana Chapman, and Kaley Warner Klemp, 2015

The Toyota Way to Continuous Improvement: Linking Strategy and Operational Excellence to Achieve Superior Performance by Jeffrey K. Liker and James K. Franz, 2011

PRINCIPLE 4: EMBRACE PROBLEMS AND WEAKNESSES

Alcoholics Anonymous—Big Book 4th Edition by Alcoholics Anonymous World Services, 2002

Crucial Conversations: Tools for Talking When Stakes Are High by Kerry Patterson, Joseph Grenny, Ron McMillan, and Al Switzler, 2018

Daring Greatly: How the Courage to Be Vulnerable Transforms the Way We Live, Love, Parent, and Lead by Brené Brown, 2012

Dare to Lead: Brave Work. Tough Conversations. Whole Hearts by Brené Brown, 2018

The E-Myth Revisited: Why Most Small Businesses Don't Work and What to Do About It by Michael E. Gerber, 1995

Leadership and Self-Deception: The Secret to Transforming Relationships & Unleashing Results by The Arbinger Institute, 2024

Loving What Is: Four Questions That Can Change Your Life by Byron Katie, 2002

Observing Spirit: Evaluating Your Daily Progress on the Path to Heaven with Gurdjieff and Swedenborg by Peter Rhodes, 2005

Seinfeld, season 5, episode 22, "The Opposite," written by Larry David, Jerry Seinfeld, and Andy Cowan, 1994

PRINCIPLE 5: MODEL YOUR BUSINESS AFTER THE HUMAN FORM

Built to Last: Successful Habits of Visionary Companies by Jim Collins and Jerry I. Porras, 1994

"Dunbar's Number: Why the Theory That Humans Can Only Maintain 150 Friendships Has Withstood 30 Years of Scrutiny" by Robin Dunbar, NeuroscienceNews.com, 2021

Good to Great: Why Some Companies Make the Leap … and Others Don't by Jim Collins, 2001

Great by Choice: Uncertainty, Chaos, and Luck—Why Some Thrive Despite Them All by Jim Collins and Morten T. Hansen, 2011

If You Want It Done Right, You Don't Have to Do It Yourself!: The Power of Effective Delegation by Donna M. Genett, 2003

Man's Search for Meaning by Viktor Frankl, 1946

"Pro Sports Team, Not a Family | Reed Hastings" by Minds of Business, YouTube video, 2022

Scrum: The Art of Doing Twice the Work in Half the Time by Jeff Sutherland, 2014